FREUD

Great Thinkers on Modern Life

Brett Kahr

PEGASUS BOOKS
NEW YORK LONDON

FREUD

Pegasus Books LLC
80 Broad Street, 5th Floor
New York, NY 10004

ISBN: 978-1-60598-677-7

10 9 8 7 8 6 5 4 3 2 1

Printed in the United States of America
Distributed by W. W. Norton & Company, Inc.

THE SCHOOL OF LIFE is dedicated to exploring life's big questions: *How can we fulfil our potential? Can work be inspiring? Why does community matter? Can relationships last a lifetime?* We don't have all the answers, but we will direct you towards a variety of useful ideas – from philosophy to literature, psychology to the visual arts – that are guaranteed to stimulate, provoke, nourish and console.

THESCHOOLOFLIFE.COM

By the same author:

D.W. Winnicott: A Biographical Portrait
Forensic Psychotherapy and Psychopathology
Exhibitionism
The Legacy of Winnicott: Essays on Infant and Child Mental Health
Sex and the Psyche
Who's Been Sleeping in Your Head?: The Secret World of Sexual Fantasies

By Sigmund Freud:

Books:

Studies on Hysteria (co-authored by Josef Breuer)
The Interpretation of Dreams
The Psychopathology of Everyday Life: Forgetting, Slips of the Tongue, Bungled Actions, Superstitions and Errors
Jokes and Their Relation to the Unconscious
Civilization and its Discontents

Essays:

'On the Psychical Mechanism of Hysterical Phenomena: A Lecture'
'Fragment of an Analysis of a Case of Hysteria'
'A Special Type of Choice of Object Made by Men: (Contributions to the Psychology of Love I)'
'On Narcissism: An Introduction'
'Some Character-Types Met with in Psycho-Analytic Work'
'A Childhood Recollection from *Dichtung und Wahrheit*'
'A Difficulty in the Path of Psycho-Analysis'
'A Disturbance of Memory on the Acropolis'
'Constructions in Analysis'

For Luca and Rafe,

*in the hope that they may find these
lessons of use one day*

CONTENTS

INTRODUCTION

....

Only days after arriving at university as a fresh-faced student, I found myself in the Senior Common Room, clutching a glass of Jerez sherry, at a Fresher's Week drinks party with the faculty. After chatting first with a medieval historian, and then with a professor of ancient Greek, I became ensconced in conversation with an eminent biochemist. 'Freud,' he bellowed, 'you're interested in Freud?' 'Yes,' I mumbled, clearly betraying all the naivety and ignorance of a fledgling, trainee psychologist. 'Hunh,' he smirked contemptuously, spilling drops of his third or fourth glass of sherry as he pontificated. 'Fifty per cent of everything that Freud wrote is completely wrong . . . and the other fifty per cent is just plain common sense.' Feebly, I attempted to argue my case that Freud might, perhaps, have some merit, but to no avail. This distinguished gentleman had resolutely made up his mind. Freud did not qualify as a proper scientist. Disconsolate, I left the party, worried that my youthful admiration for Freud might be dangerously misguided.

Any jibes that I had to navigate in the 1980s rather pale by comparison with what Sigmund Freud had to endure during the first decades of the twentieth century. A neurologist by training, Freud specialized in the treatment of nervous diseases such as hysteria and anxiety neurosis; and as a young doctor, he shocked the Viennese medical establishment with his observations that many psychologically unwell people might have suffered from traumatic experiences in infancy and childhood, often of a sexual nature. Freud wrote about these traumas in graphic detail, avoiding the euphemisms regularly deployed in late-nineteenth-century discourse. This remarkable frankness caused many senior physicians to lambaste Freud as little more than a sexually perverse lunatic.

When Freud died in 1939, Mr Andrew Rugg-Gunn, a Senior Surgeon at the Western Ophthalmic Hospital in London, attacked the dead psychoanalyst in the pages of the venerable medical journal *The Lancet*, exclaiming that 'Freud's unhealthy obsession with sex has been responsible to an overwhelming extent for the depravity of mind and perversity of taste that has affected, among others, English people and particularly English women since the last war. In itself a sufficiently grave evil, this result has had consequences immeasurably malignant, for it undoubtedly paved the way for wide acceptance of that complete Jewish ideology out of which sprang bolshevism, nazism and the present war.' But *The Lancet* also published an encomium written by Dr John Rickman, one of Freud's earliest British disciples, who claimed that Freud 'made one feel to be in the company of a new kind of being – an ideal for human nature'. Clearly, Freud has evoked a great range of responses, from those who have come to regard him as the most important psychologist in history, to those who have ridiculed him as an obsessive, lascivious charlatan.

Born on 6 May 1856, in Freiberg, Moravia, part of the sprawling Austro-Hungarian empire, Sigismund Schlomo Freud grew up in a relatively impecunious home, the son of a struggling wool merchant and his wife. In 1859, the family moved to Vienna, where the young Freud distinguished himself academically. Shortly before he graduated from school, Freud changed his name from the Hebraic Sigismund Schlomo to the more Germanic 'Sigmund', both as an expression of his wish to avoid, as much as he could, the regnant anti-Semitism of the period, and to pronounce, with Wagnerian bravado, his knightly intentions. Sigmund Freud would not be a struggling merchant like his father. He would attend the Universität zu Wien (University of Vienna), the ancient seat of learning founded in 1365, and would become a physician.

Freud qualified successfully as a medical doctor in 1881, and shortly thereafter, he joined staff of the Allgemeines Krankenhaus, Vienna's premier hospital. Also at this time, he made the acquaintance of a prominent, more senior physician, Dr Josef Breuer, who told Freud about his extraordinary treatment of a young

Viennese lady, Bertha Pappenheim, who suffered from a host of puzzling hysterical symptoms such as visual hallucinations and unexplained paralyses. Whereas other doctors of the period would prescribe sedatives, or rest cures, or hot baths, or, indeed, no treatment at all, for their hysterical patients, Breuer began to have *conversations* with Fräulein Pappenheim. Surprisingly, simply by *talking*, her symptoms began to disappear, prompting the young woman to refer to this process as 'chimney sweeping', or as the 'talking cure'. Dr Breuer's account of this work impressed Freud hugely and taught him a great deal about the treatability of the neuroses, those psychological disorders which seemed to have no obvious physical cause, and which did not respond wholly to conventional somatic treatments.

Most nineteenth-century physicians regarded hysterical neurotics as silly, hyperemotional society women. Today, we might refer to them, somewhat unkindly, as 'drama queens'. But Freud began to look beyond their attention-seeking behaviours, suspecting that these women suffered from deeper concerns. In order to improve his knowledge of hysteria and the other psychoneuroses, he spent several months in Paris at the Salpêtrière hospital, working with France's leading neurologist and hysteria specialist, Professeur Jean-Martin Charcot, who taught Freud that men, too, could suffer from hysteria, and, even more importantly, that the symptoms of hysteria could be cured through hypnosis. Vitally, the young Sigmund Freud had now come to appreciate that neurosis need not be a permanent, crippling condition; the illness could, in fact, be ameliorated, albeit not by *medical* means, but, rather, by *psychological* methods.

Upon his return to Vienna, Freud opened his own private practice on Easter Sunday 1886, deploying the newfangled 'talking cure' that he had learned from Breuer, and the hypnotic procedures that he had absorbed from Charcot and others (eventually abandoning the latter technique, and concentrating on the development of the former). One of his patients, a woman called Madame Benvenisti, must have found her treatment with Freud helpful, and in thanks, she gave him a couch as a present. Freud soon began to encourage his patients to lie on this comfortable divan, and he then seated himself behind the couch – out of sight – which allowed his patients to speak about their private fears and fantasies, their memories and desires, their sexual and aggressive impulses, and their dreams and symptoms, in a less inhibited manner. To his astonishment and delight, the talking cure proved exceptionally powerful, and Freud began to achieve impressive results. His patients began to articulate their traumas, and as a consequence, they experienced freedom and relief for the first time. While most of the Viennese danced to the light-hearted waltzes of Johann Strauss the Younger, which helped them to forget their troubles, Freud forced the Viennese to remember, and he created a unique setting in which they could do so.

It would be anti-historical to suppose that Freud burst onto the psychiatric scene as Athena from the skull of Zeus. Other physicians in Vienna, and on the Continent, had also begun to undertake work of a similar nature; indeed, much of fin-de-siècle Vienna brimmed with the excitement of new ideas not only in medicine, but also in politics and in the arts; and by the turn of the twentieth century, the Austrian capital had become a breeding ground for revolutionary ideas, whether in the drawings of Egon Schiele, who defied convention with his sketches of bare, corpse-like figures; whether in the music of Arnold Schönberg, who introduced atonality; or whether in the plays of Arthur Schnitzler, who wrote about sexuality with great explicitness. Freud formed only a part of this swirling climate of creativity, of liberalism and of provocation, albeit quite an important part.

In 1895, Freud and Breuer published a book about their 'talking cure' for hysteria, a monograph which launched Freud as a growing presence on the international medical stage. Shortly after publication, one Alfred von Berger described Freud's new psychological treatment in a Viennese newspaper as '*Seelenchirurgie*' ('soul surgery'), brilliantly encapsulating Freudian therapy as a new form of medicine, which treated not the body but, rather, the mind. The next year, in 1896, Freud introduced the term *'psycho-analyse'* (psychoanalysis) for the first time, in French, in a neurological journal. An impressive stream of publications followed thereafter, among them the famous *Die Traumdeutung* (*The Interpretation of Dreams*), which appeared on 4 November 1899, but which bore the date 1900 on its title page, indicative of the publisher's recognition of this book as a vital new work for a daring new century. This magnum opus not only revealed the fruits of Freud's intensive study of the dream as a deeply meaningful part of one's mental life, but it also provided a carefully reasoned, intricately articulated model of the functioning of the human psyche; one which consists of a conscious mind, somewhat restricted in size, as well as an unconscious mind, quite cavernous by comparison, which governs most of our thoughts, outside of our conscious awareness.

A shrewd businessman and publicist as well as a conscientious scientist and prolific author, Freud knew that he would have to 'market' his psychoanalytical treatment, and that in order to infiltrate the psychiatric establishment, he would need to publish books and essays on his method, and train younger workers in the psychoanalytical art who could confirm his findings about the efficacy of the talking cure. After decades of unceasing toil, psychoanalysis eventually became so popular that it began to penetrate mainstream culture. In 1926, Georg Wilhelm Pabst, the noted silent filmmaker, released his movie *Geheimnisse einer Seele* (*Secrets of a Soul*) in Berlin, which dramatized the fictitious story of a man who underwent psychoanalytical treatment for a knife phobia. And on Broadway, that same year, the rising songwriters Richard Rodgers and Lorenz Hart created a new musical, *Peggy-Ann*, which contained many references to the new Freudian psychology, and which included an extended dream sequence.

Clearly, Freud had arrived. But so, too, had the *Nazionalsozialistische Deutsche Arbeiterpartei*, who quickly identified Freud as a subversive Jew who not only wrote filthy sex books, but whose very philosophy implied that people could dare to take control of their own lives by undergoing psychoanalysis – clearly the very antithesis of the Hitlerian ideology of subordination to a fascist state. And so, in 1933, the Nazis burned Freud's books in a huge bonfire in Berlin's Opernplatz, along with the writings of other Jews such as Karl Marx and Albert Einstein. In spite of pleadings from his colleagues, Freud refused to emigrate from his Austrian homeland; but finally in 1938, after the Nazis had interrogated two of his children, he relented, and with assistance from his wealthy disciple, the French princess Marie Bonaparte, who bribed the Nazis, Freud fled with his family to safety in London, where he spent the last fifteen-and-a-half months of his life. Riddled with cancer of the jaw, Freud died at the age of eighty-three years on 23 September 1939, from an overdose of morphine – administered by his physician, to ease the unbearable physical pain.

The life and work of Freud has held an unwavering fascination for me ever since my teenage years. As I persevered with my own training in psychology and in psychotherapy, I continued to read Freud with increasing engagement. Not only did I become a practitioner of Freudian psychotherapy and have continued to work in this field for the last three decades, but I myself also underwent a long period of Freudian psychoanalysis which I found to be an extremely beneficial experience in so many respects. Additionally, I trained as a historian, and in this role I have interviewed a small number of people who had had personal contact with Freud, as well as a large number of people (several hundred, in fact) who had worked with Freud's earliest disciples. As a young man, I even spent a year working in Freud's house in London – now the Freud Museum – and more recently, I returned to serve as one of the museum's trustees. I confess, therefore, that I have a strong bias towards Freud, but one formed, I hope, from a lifetime of serious study of his contributions. As a clinician, I find Freud absolutely indispensable, and I take Freud with me into my consulting room on a daily basis, for he has furnished both me and my colleagues with the essential tools for understanding the origins and the treatment of psychological misery and madness.

Although I have enjoyed a scholarly and professional love affair with Freud, it would not be at all correct to suppose that I idealize him, or that I have remained blind to his foibles, his vulnerabilities, or even to his occasional cruelties of character. Freud could be deeply warm and generous to patients, highly brilliant in his scientific work, and extremely imaginative in his capacity to turn his psychological insights into an international movement of psychoanalytical practitioners. But he could also be callous and ruthless, and, in a small number of instances, even professionally unethical. As the decades have unfolded, I trust that I have acquired a well-rounded insight into Freud's life and work, which has allowed me to be highly appreciative as well as appropriately cautious. I have learned a great deal from Freud about how to live a good life, but I have also absorbed many object lessons on how to behave rather differently.

1

HOW TO SABOTAGE
YOUR GREATEST SUCCESS

....

In 1994, the movie *Four Weddings and a Funeral* burst onto cinema screens, and soon became the highest-grossing British film of all time, earning an Academy Award nomination for Best Picture. Hugh Grant, the film's leading actor, received a handful of prestigious awards and catapulted to international stardom, signing a deal with the American motion-picture company Castle Rock Entertainment, then owned by media mogul Ted Turner. Grant subsequently starred in his first major Hollywood movie, the comedy *Nine Months*. But literally two-and-a-half weeks before the film's release, the Los Angeles Police arrested Mr Grant for lewd public conduct with a prostitute called Divine Brown.

One could cite numerous comparable stories of men and women who, shortly after achieving great fame or success, managed somehow to sabotage their achievements, oftentimes in spectacularly humiliating and self-destructive ways. Eliot Spitzer, for example, the much-admired Governor of the State of

New York, became embroiled in a sex scandal soon after his election and, consequently, damaged his gubernatorial career.

The news of Hugh Grant's arrest baffled millions: how could the adorable, charming, well-bred, almost aristocratic Hugh Grant, envied by men the world over for his sexy girlfriend Elizabeth Hurley, find himself in flagrante with a sex worker who charged him, reputedly, $60, thus jeopardizing his relationship, his livelihood and his reputation? Likewise, how could Eliot Spitzer, renowned for his libertarian political work fighting white-collar crime, end up in a similar situation?

These success-spoiling scandals would not have surprised Sigmund Freud. After many years of working psychoanalytically with neurotic patients, Freud had come to appreciate that people often suffer breakdowns and explosions in their private lives not after a *failure* but, paradoxically, after a *triumph*. In a classic essay, Freud endeavoured to explain the dangers of success:

> Psycho-analytic work has furnished us with the thesis that people fall ill of a neurosis as a result of *frustration*. What is meant is the frustration of the satisfaction of their libidinal wishes, and some digression is necessary in order to make the thesis intelligible. For a neurosis to be generated there

must be a conflict between a person's libidinal wishes and the part of his personality we call his ego, which is the expression of his instinct of self-preservation and which also includes his *ideals* of his personality. A pathogenic conflict of this kind takes place only when the libido tries to follow paths and aims which the ego has long since overcome and condemned and has therefore prohibited for ever; and this the libido only does if it is deprived of the possibility of an ideal ego-syntonic satisfaction. Hence privation, frustration of a real satisfaction, is the first condition for the generation of a neurosis, although, indeed, it is far from being the only one.

So much the more surprising, and indeed bewildering, must it appear when as a doctor one makes the discovery that people occasionally fall ill precisely when a deeply-rooted and long-cherished wish has come to fulfilment. It seems then as though they were not able to tolerate their happiness; for there can be no question that there is a causal connection between their success and their falling ill.

I had an opportunity of obtaining an insight into a woman's history, which I propose to describe as typical of these tragic occurrences. She was of good birth and well brought-up, but as quite a young girl she could not restrain her zest for life; she ran away from home and roved about the world in search of adventures, till she made the acquaintance of an artist who could appreciate her feminine charms but could also divine, in spite of what she had fallen to, the finer qualities she possessed. He took her to live with him, and she proved a faithful companion to him, and seemed only to need social rehabilitation to achieve complete happiness. After many years of life together, he succeeded in getting his family reconciled to her, and was then prepared to make her his legal wife. At that moment she began to go to pieces. She neglected the house of which she was now about to become the rightful mistress, imagined herself persecuted by his relatives, who wanted to take her into the family, debarred her lover, through her senseless jealousy, from all social intercourse, hindered him in his artistic work, and soon succumbed to an incurable mental illness.

On another occasion I came across the case of a most respectable man who, himself an academic teacher, had for many years cherished the natural wish to succeed the master who had initiated him into his own studies. When this older man retired, and his colleagues informed him that it was he who was chosen as successor, he began to hesitate, depreciated his merits, declared himself unworthy to fill the position designed for him, and fell into a melancholia which unfitted him for all activity for some years.

> Different as these two cases are in other respects, they yet agree in this one point: the illness followed close upon the fulfilment of a wish and put an end to all enjoyment of it.
>
> ('Some Character-Types Met with in Psycho-Analytic Work', 1916)

Some twenty years later, in 1936, Freud revisited this theme in a letter to the French writer Romain Rolland, in which he described his sense of unreality when, in middle age, Freud had stood with his brother atop the Acropolis in Athens, surprised and disbelieving, and curiously disturbed by the experience, discovering that the Acropolis really *does* exist.

> As a rule people fall ill as a result of frustration, of the non-fulfilment of some vital necessity or desire. But with these people the opposite is the case; they fall ill, or even go entirely to pieces, because an overwhelmingly powerful wish of theirs has been fulfilled. But the contrast between the two situations is not so great as it seems at first. What happens in the paradoxical case is merely that the place of the external frustration is taken by an internal one. The sufferer does not permit himself happiness: the internal frustration commands him to cling to the external one. But why? Because – so runs the answer in a number of cases – one cannot expect

Fate to grant one anything so good. In fact, another instance of 'too good to be true', the expression of a pessimism of which a large portion seems to find a home in many of us. In another set of cases, just as in those who are wrecked by success, we find a sense of guilt or inferiority, which can be translated: 'I'm not worthy of such happiness, I don't deserve it.'

. . .

But precisely my own experience on the Acropolis, which actually culminated in a disturbance of memory and a falsification of the past, helps us to demonstrate this connection. It is not true that in my schooldays I ever doubted the real existence of Athens. I only doubted whether I should ever see Athens. It seemed to me beyond the realms of possibility that I should travel so far – that I should 'go such a long way'. This was linked up with the limitations and poverty of our conditions of life in my youth. My longing to travel was no doubt also the expression of a wish to escape from that pressure, like the force which drives so many adolescent children to run away from home. I had long seen clearly that a great part of the pleasure of travel lies in the fulfilment of these early wishes – that it is rooted, that is, in dissatisfaction with home and family. When first one catches sight of the sea, crosses the ocean and experiences as realities cities and lands which for so long had been distant, unattainable things of desire

– one feels oneself like a hero who has performed deeds of improbable greatness. I might that day on the Acropolis have said to my brother: Do you still remember how, when we were young, we used day after day to walk along the same streets on our way to school, and how every Sunday we used to go to the Prater or on some excursion we knew so well? And now, here we are in Athens, and standing on the Acropolis! We really *have* gone a long way!' So too, if I may compare such a small event with a greater one, Napoleon, during his coronation as Emperor in Notre Dame, turned to one of his brothers – it must no doubt have been the eldest one, Joseph – and remarked: 'What would *Monsieur notre Père* have said to this, if he could have been here to-day?'.

But here we come upon the solution of the little problem of why it was that already at Trieste we interfered with our enjoyment of the voyage to Athens. It must be that a sense of guilt was attached to the satisfaction in having gone such a long way: there was something about it that was wrong, that from earliest times had been forbidden. It was something to do with a child's criticism of his father, with the undervaluation which took the place of the overvaluation of earlier childhood. It seems as though the essence of success was to have got further than one's father, and as though to excel one's father was still something forbidden.

As an addition to this generally valid motive there was a special factor present in our particular case. The very theme of Athens and the Acropolis in itself contained evidence of the son's superiority. Our father had been in business, he had had no secondary education, and Athens could not have meant much to him. Thus what interfered with our enjoyment of the journey to Athens was a feeling of *filial piety*.

('A Disturbance of Memory on the Acropolis', 1936)

Freud came to understand that when we triumph over our parents, or believe that we have done so, by becoming richer, more fertile, more successful, or even by living better lives or longer lives than they had done, we experience an aching sense of guilt that we have hurt or shamed our parents. And also, we fear that our parents might attack us, in consequence, as a way of managing their own enviousness. Of course, Freud suspected that these processes occur unconsciously. In his own self-analytical investigation, he hypothesized that he had experienced such a peculiar sensation when he reached the Acropolis because he knew that his relatively uneducated and impoverished father, the wool merchant Jakob Freud, had never achieved such heights; hence Sigmund Freud still regarded himself as having done something dangerous and cruel to his father, in spite of the fact that his father had died years previously.

Freud never denied that frustration of our wishes causes suffering. Of course we will be unhappy if we fail to receive a promotion, if our partner leaves us, or if our children disappoint us in some way. But Freud introduced a new idea into psychology, namely, that we all have the serious potential to become disturbed when our wishes *do* come true, not because we struggle to know what to do with our newly acquired status or wealth but, rather, because we fear that we have damaged our parents in some way.

By highlighting the fear of success, Freud has bequeathed to us a very important life lesson. When we do something spectacular, whether on the world stage, or in a more modest way by marrying our sweetheart, giving birth to a baby, or even finishing that damned report for the boss at work, we have the opportunity to experience joy and relief on the *conscious* level, but on the *unconscious* level we may, in fact, be at risk; hence we should be vigilant, and so too should our nearest and dearest. Therefore, when our recently promoted spouse suggests that he or she might want to take up skydiving, lion-taming, or alligator-wrestling, as a good use of the newly acquired spare cash at hand, we might just wish to suggest an alternative.

2

HOW TO MAKE A MOUNTAIN
OUT OF A MOLEHILL

....

In 1938, Sigmund Freud and his family fled from the Nazi menace in Austria, and sought refuge in London. Freud spent the last year of his life in a beautiful house in Swiss Cottage which became transformed into the Freud Museum in 1986. As a very young man, I had the privilege of working at the museum for a year shortly after it opened to the public. Of course we had a gift shop, like all museums, selling postcards of Freud's couch and other such items; and we prided ourselves upon having an extremely tasteful shop.

To everyone's great consternation, word had reached us at the Freud Museum that Dr Kurt Eissler, a Viennese-émigré psychoanalyst living in New York City (and for decades the world's premier Freud scholar), had accused us of selling Freud T-shirts. Worse still, someone had apparently told Dr Eissler that the gift shop stocked not only Freud T-shirts but also Freudian *slippers* – an amusing idea in view of Freud's famous work on slips of the tongue, better known as Freudian *slips*. The Director of the Freud

Museum sent a note to Dr Eissler reassuring him that we would never dare to be so crass as to sell either T-shirts or slippers emblazoned with Freud's steely visage and cigar-filled fist.

Twenty-five years later, I returned to the Freud Museum to serve as a trustee. And I can cheerfully report that nowadays we *do* sell stylish Freud T-shirts and comfy Freudian slippers; and perhaps, if memory serves me correctly, the shop has even sold actual Freudian lingerie (or Freudian 'slips') from time to time. And no one seems to mind.

We have all heard about Freudian slips – those moments when we trip over our tongue, or when we forget something of no apparent consequence. But how exactly might we define Freudian slips, and should we make a big deal out of them, as Dr Kurt Eissler had done? Should we even parade them proudly across our chests or on our feet? Let us begin with a few brief exemplars.

'Rupert', a young patient who had come to see me for psychotherapy, had a quandary. He had spent the last six months dating a woman called Sally, and although he had an explosively satisfying sexual life with this buxom blonde, he found her quite boring out of bed, quite poorly educated and quite inane, calling her 'a real airhead'. One day, Rupert came to his session laughing ironically. He told me that he had at last decided to break up with Sally, explaining that he had recently sent her an email in which he found himself writing 'Dear *Silly*' instead of 'Dear *Sally*'. Rupert knew enough about psychoanalysis to realize that he had made a Freudian slip. 'You know,' he reflected, 'I think my Freudian slip is significant. The letter "a" in "Sally" is all the way on the left-hand side of the keyboard, and the letter "i" in "Silly" is in the middle. This can't have been an accident. I suppose my unconscious mind told me what I really think about her.'

Years ago, an American colleague, Professor Herbert Strean, a noted psychoanalyst who bore the title of Distinguished Professor at Rutgers University in New Jersey, appeared on television to discuss his work. The interviewer, deeply hostile to psychoanalysis, introduced Strean – quite unconsciously – as 'Disgusting Professor' at the university. One need not be a Freud specialist to appreciate that seemingly innocent slips of the tongue may not be quite so innocent after all.

Let us consider one further instance of a Freudian slip, this time the slip of a psychiatrist. Some years ago, I attended a professional conference, and found myself in conversation with an old friend, whom I shall call Dr Brinker. Suddenly, Brinker's ex-girlfriend, a beautiful child psychotherapist, walked by us, with a good-looking man (a noted psychiatrist) on her arm. Dr Brinker's former lover waved at us, smiled, and then disappeared into the crowd. Brinker looked wistful and commented: 'You know she's married to that guy, don't you? Silverman's his name. We were medical students together years and years ago. I hope they'll be very happy.' Privately I gulped, and I did not have the heart to tell him that I knew the other psychiatrist well enough to know that Dr Brinker had made a serious slip of the tongue, without realizing that he had done so. He had in fact misremembered the name of the new man. His real name was not Silverman at all, but Goldman. Indeed, Brinker had taken the name of his more successful sexual rival and, with a quiet slip of the tongue, had downgraded him from *gold* to *silver*.

Freud regarded such seemingly trivial linguistic infelicities as vital to our understanding of the human mind. In his famous monograph, published originally as two journal articles in 1901, and then in book form in 1904, he observed:

> The ordinary [linguistic] material which we use for talking in our native language appears to be protected against being forgotten; but it succumbs all the more frequently to another disturbance, which is known as a 'slip of the tongue'.
>
> *(The Psychopathology of Everyday Life: Forgetting, Slips of the Tongue, Bungled Actions, Superstitions and Errors, 1901)*

Freud then furnished his readers with a welter of clinical illustrations of these slips of the tongue, which have come to be known in technical psychoanalytical vocabulary as 'parapraxes', a fabricated term derived from ancient Greek. Freud had witnessed many instances of 'Sally' becoming 'Silly', and 'Goldman' becoming 'Silverman':

When I asked another woman patient at the end of the session how her uncle was, she answered: 'I don't know, nowadays I only see him *in flagranti.*' Next day she began: 'I am really ashamed of myself for having given you such a stupid answer. You must of course have thought me a very uneducated person who is always getting foreign words mixed up. I meant to say: *en passant.*' We did not as yet know the source of the foreign phrase which she had wrongly applied. In the same session, however, while continuing the previous day's topic, she brought up a reminiscence in which the chief role was played by being caught *in flagranti.* The slip of the tongue of the day before had therefore anticipated the memory which at the time had not yet become conscious.

(The Psychopathology of Everyday Life: Forgetting, Slips of the Tongue, Bungled Actions, Superstitions and Errors, 1901)

In a later edition of this text, published in 1920, Freud offered the following rich vignette of a slip of the pen (a variant of slip of the tongue), which contained quite deadly marital undertones:

> An American living in Europe who had left his wife on bad terms felt that he could now effect a reconciliation with her, and asked her to come across the Atlantic and join him on a certain date. 'It would be fine,' he wrote, 'if you could come on the *Mauretania* as I did.' He did not however dare to send the sheet of paper which had this sentence on it. He preferred to write it out again. For he did not want her to notice how he had had to correct the name of the ship. He had first written '*Lusitania*'.
>
> This slip of the pen needs no explanation: its interpretation is perfectly plain. But a happy chance enables a further point to be added. Before the war his wife paid her first visit to Europe after the death of her only sister. If I am not mistaken, the *Mauretania* is the surviving sister-ship of the *Lusitania*, which was sunk in the war.
>
> *(The Psychopathology of Everyday Life: Forgetting, Slips of the Tongue, Bungled Actions, Superstitions and Errors, 1901)*

Thus, we begin to understand that a slip of the tongue might reveal repressed hostility (for example, 'Silly' versus 'Sally'), or even fully fledged unconscious death wishes ('*Lusitania*' versus '*Mauretania*'), which might need to be brought to consciousness. Freud explained further:

In the psychotherapeutic procedure which I employ for resolving and removing neurotic symptoms I am very often faced with the task of discovering, from the patient's apparently casual utterances and associations, a thought-content which is at pains to remain concealed but which cannot nevertheless avoid unintentionally betraying its existence in a whole variety of ways. Slips of the tongue often perform a most valuable service here, as I could show by some highly convincing and at the same time very singular examples. Thus, for instance, a patient will be speaking of his aunt and, without noticing the slip, will consistently call her 'my mother'; or another will refer to her husband as her 'brother'. In this way they draw my attention to the fact that they have 'identified' these persons with one another – that they have put them into a series which implies a recurrence of the same type in their emotional life. – To give another example: a young man of twenty introduced himself to me during my consulting hours in these words: 'I am the father of So-and-so who came to you for treatment. I beg your pardon, I meant to say I am his brother: he is four years older than I am.' I inferred that he intended this slip to express the view that, like his brother, he had fallen ill through the fault of his father; that, like his brother, he wished to be cured; but that his father was the one who most needed to be cured. – At other times an arrangement of words that sounds unusual, or an expression that seems forced, is enough to reveal that a repressed thought is participating in the patient's remarks, which had a different end in view.

. . .

I still secretly cling to my expectation that even apparently simple slips of the tongue could be traced to interference by a half-suppressed idea that lies *outside* the intended context.

(The Psychopathology of Everyday Life: Forgetting, Slips of the Tongue, Bungled Actions, Superstitions and Errors, 1901)

In summarizing his findings, based on a careful analysis of more than 300 pages of detailed parapraxes, Freud opined:

The general conclusion that emerges from the previous individual discussions may be stated in the following terms. *Certain shortcomings in our psychical functioning* – whose common characteristics will in a moment be defined more closely – *and certain seemingly unintentional performances prove, if psycho-analytic methods of investigation are applied to them, to have valid motives and to be determined by motives unknown to consciousness.*

In order to be included in the class of phenomena explicable in this way, a psychical parapraxis must fulfil the following conditions:

a. It must not exceed certain dimensions fixed by our judgement, which we characterize by the expression 'within the limits of the normal'.

b. It must be in the nature of a momentary and temporary disturbance. The same function must have been performed by us more correctly before, or we must at all times believe ourselves capable of carrying it out more correctly. If we are corrected by someone else, we must at once recognize the rightness of the correction and the wrongness of our own psychical process.

c. If we perceive the parapraxis at all, we must not be aware in ourselves of any motive for it. We must rather be tempted to explain it by 'inattentiveness', or to put it down to 'chance'.

(The Psychopathology of Everyday Life: Forgetting, Slips of the Tongue, Bungled Actions, Superstitions and Errors, 1901)

But although Freud recognized that slips of the tongue and slips of the pen might be very meaningful, one must be cautious about making important life decisions solely on the basis of the Freudian slip:

I do not believe that an event in whose occurrence my mental life plays no part can teach me any hidden thing about the future shape of reality; but I believe that an unintentional manifestation of my own mental activity *does* on the other hand disclose something hidden, though again it is something that belongs only to my mental life [not to external reality]. I believe in external (real) chance, it is true, but not in internal (psychical) accidental events.

. . .

But there is one thing which the severest and the mildest cases all have in common, and which is equally found in parapraxes and chance actions: *the phenomena can be traced back to incompletely suppressed psychical material, which, although pushed away by consciousness, has nevertheless not been robbed of all capacity for expressing itself.*

(*The Psychopathology of Everyday Life: Forgetting, Slips of the Tongue, Bungled Actions, Superstitions and Errors*, 1901)

So, has Sigmund Freud made a mountain out of a molehill? Should we regard our 'Silly's as merely insignificant distortions of 'Sally's, or might we find that such linguistic inaccuracies come to represent deeply important eruptions of unprocessed, unknown, unconscious material from the hidden depths of our mind? I recommend that we should all listen carefully to our speech, and pay heed to our writing, and even to our rapid-fire text-messaging. In this era of spellcheck and autocorrect, perhaps we have found a way to sanitize our language so quickly that some of our most important communications to our own selves may become lost in the mists of cyberspace.

3

HOW TO BETRAY
A DEEP, DARK SECRET

....

In 1885 Sigmund Freud, then twenty-nine years old, received a travel bursary to study in Paris under the legendary French neurologist, Professeur Jean-Martin Charcot, known to many as the 'Napoleon of the neuroses'. Charcot taught Freud a great deal about psychological illness, not least that many people become neurotic as a result of difficulties in their sexual lives, which Charcot had described as the *secrets d'alcôve* ('secrets of the bedchamber'). Building upon Charcot's clinical observations, Freud returned to Vienna some months later, and opened a private practice, specializing in nervous cases. He soon came to appreciate the accuracy of Charcot's pronouncement, and before long, he encountered many patients suffering from a raft of psychological difficulties, many of whom had experienced sexual traumas or sexual guilt. We must remember, of course, that Freud worked at a time when even physicians regarded masturbation, premarital sexuality and homosexuality as perverse. Fortunately, Freud had the capacity to listen to his patients' sexual anxieties and sexual secrets in a non-judgemental way, and he soon discovered that after talking, the patients experienced a catharsis and a relief from their depressions, anxieties and other disturbing symptoms.

With great clinical sensitivity, Freud realized that many of his patients had never before revealed their sexual secrets to another living soul. They found their *secrets d'alcôve* far too embarrassing, far too shameful, far too disgusting. He knew that his patients would reveal their most horrifying confessions only if he could guarantee them absolute confidentiality, promising not to reveal their stories to any third party. Freud thus became the supreme diplomat, and he imbued his psychoanalytical philosophy with a veneration of privacy. He even constructed a separate entrance and a separate exit to his consulting room so that his patients would never meet one another in the waiting room.

As a physician who had spent many years working as a researcher in the fields of physiology, histology and anatomy, Freud knew that in order to share his new discoveries about the sexual origins of the neuroses, he would have to publish his case histories. But as a man who had sworn a Hippocratic oath, and as someone who recognized that he would have to be supremely careful and confidential with his patients' stories, he also knew that he would have to disguise his patients' true identities – a radical notion at a time in medical history when many other physicians revealed their patients' real names liberally in professional periodicals. In 1905, Freud published a monograph about a young woman suffering from hysteria, in which he observed:

If it is true that the causes of hysterical disorders are to be found in the intimacies of the patients' psychosexual life, and that hysterical symptoms are the expression of their most secret and repressed wishes, then the complete elucidation of a case of hysteria is bound to involve the revelation of those intimacies and the betrayal of those secrets. It is certain that the patients would never have spoken if it had occurred to them that their admissions might possibly be put to scientific uses; and it is equally certain that to ask them themselves for leave to publish their case would be quite unavailing. In such circumstances persons of delicacy, as well as those who were merely timid, would give first place to the duty of medical discretion and would declare with regret that the matter was one upon which they could offer science no enlightenment. But in my opinion the physician has taken upon himself duties not only towards the individual patient but towards science as well; and his duties towards science mean ultimately nothing else than his duties towards the many other patients who are suffering or will some day suffer from the same disorder. Thus it becomes the physician's duty to publish what he believes he knows of the causes and structure of hysteria, and it becomes a disgraceful piece of cowardice on his part to neglect doing so, as long as he can avoid causing direct personal injury to the single patient concerned.

('Fragment of an Analysis of
a Case of Hysteria', 1905)

Cleverly, Freud had managed to have his cake and to eat it too. He knew that he would have to preserve the privacy of his patients, but he also realized that he needed to serve science, and that he would need to find a means of publishing his findings. And so he adopted a policy of changing the names of his patients and disguising other key, potentially identifiable details of their biographies, in the hope of protecting their anonymity. In this respect, he became a practitioner of delicacy, of discretion and, one might propose, of diplomacy as well.

Freud chose a fictitious name, 'Dora', to describe his young hysterical patient. He continued:

I think I have taken every precaution to prevent my patient from suffering any such injury. I have picked out a person the scenes of whose life were laid not in Vienna but in a remote provincial town, and whose personal circumstances must there-fore be practically unknown in Vienna. I have from the very beginning kept the fact of her being under my treatment such a careful secret that only one other physician – and one in whose discretion I have complete confidence – can be aware that the girl was a patient of mine. I have waited for four whole years since the end of the treatment and have postponed publication till hearing that a change has taken place in the patient's life of such a character as allows me to suppose that her own interest in the occurrences and psychological events which are to be related here may now have grown faint. Needless to say, I have allowed no name to stand which could put a non-medical reader upon the scent; and the publication of the case in a purely scientific and technical periodical should, further, afford a guarantee against unauthorized readers of this sort. I naturally cannot prevent the patient herself from being pained if her own case history should accidentally fall into her hands. But she will learn nothing from it that she does not already know; and she may ask herself who besides her could discover from it that she is the subject of this paper.

('Fragment of an Analysis of a
Case of Hysteria', 1905)

As a young girl, Dora experienced a traumatic shock. An older man, whom Freud had called Herr K. – a friend of Dora's father – had made sexual advances towards her. Today, we would regard such transgenerational contact as sexual abuse. But Dora did not know about ChildLine or social services. She regarded this as a shameful secret which she had told to no one until she had met Freud:

> The experience with Herr K. – his making love to her and the insult to her honour which was involved – seems to provide in Dora's case the psychical trauma which Breuer and I declared long ago to be the indispensable prerequisite for the production of a hysterical disorder.
>
> . . .
>
> When the first difficulties of the treatment had been overcome, Dora told me of an earlier episode with Herr K., which was even better calculated to act as a sexual trauma. She was fourteen years old at the time. Herr K. had made an arrangement with her and his wife that they should meet him one afternoon at his place of business in the principal square of B – so as to have a view of a church festival. He persuaded his wife, however, to stay at home, and sent away his clerks, so that he was alone when the girl arrived. When the time for the procession approached, he asked the girl to wait for him at the door which opened on to the staircase leading to the upper story, while he pulled down the outside shutters. He then came back, and, instead of going out by the open door, suddenly clasped the girl to him and pressed a kiss upon her lips. This was surely

just the situation to call up a distinct feeling of sexual excitement in a girl of fourteen who had never before been approached. But Dora had at that moment a violent feeling of disgust, tore herself free from the man, and hurried past him to the staircase and from there to the street door. She nevertheless continued to meet Herr K. Neither of them ever mentioned the little scene; and according to her account Dora kept it a secret till her confession during the treatment.

('Fragment of an Analysis of a
Case of Hysteria', 1905)

Freud wrote at a time when even medical professionals knew very little about sexual trauma and abuse. In spite of this, Freud managed to create an environment in which Dora could dare to admit the ways in which an older person, Herr K., had behaved intrusively and cruelly to her. And Freud also dared to observe that such an encounter could be frightening to a teenage girl and that it might also contain elements of excitement as well; especially during the late nineteenth century when most manifestations of sexuality would be regarded as taboo. However one conceptualizes the situation, Freud succeeded in recognizing that his patients harboured aching secrets, often of a sexual nature, and that if he wished to establish a safe space in which these experiences could be discussed, then he would need to demonstrate a supremely diplomatic sensitivity to matters of confidentiality. Although Freud never attended the Court of St James's, he did, in fact, become one of the first clinical diplomats.

In 1776, Benjamin Franklin, the great patriot, statesman and inventor, became the very first American ambassador to France. A card-carrying diplomat, Franklin knew about the importance of tact and secrecy. In fact, he once opined that, 'Three may keep a secret, if two of them are dead.'

Freud, in contrast to Franklin, realized that it might be possible to respect the privacy of another human being, and that one can, in fact, preserve a secret without being dead. In 1932, an American physician called Dr Roy Grinker came to Vienna to undergo psychoanalysis with Freud. Grinker's wife Mildred worried that her husband might not have shared all his secrets with Freud – a common complaint among the spouses of psychotherapy patients – and so Grinker told his wife that if she needed confirmation about just how much he had already confessed to Freud, then she could write to him herself. When Dr Grinker then mentioned this interchange to Freud, the father of psychoanalysis replied: 'Yes, let her write to me, providing she doesn't expect me to answer the letter.'

Today we live in a world virtually devoid of privacy. The domestic lives of many people, especially celebrities and politicians, often become exposed and archived forever on the Internet. Having worked with men and women whose most personal secrets have become public property, I can confirm that the victims of such exposure suffer incredible agony. My colleagues and I in the mental health field have become particularly concerned that so many teenagers experience cyber-bullying. Several psychological professionals have, in fact, treated adolescents who have sent revealing photographs of themselves to a boyfriend or girlfriend only to discover that the so-called 'friend' had then posted the photograph on Facebook or on the Internet for the entire world to see. Many of the young people thus betrayed have required years of psychotherapy as a consequence.

In an era that no longer respects privacy, confidentiality or secrecy, we have much to learn from Freud and from those psychotherapists who have followed in his footsteps. What we hear in the consulting room remains private. In fact, what we learn about the private lives of our patients will go with us to our graves. Next time we find ourselves blurting out a friend's secret or a workmate's confidence, or the next time we drop a none-too-subtle hint about someone else's private life, perhaps we can remember the importance that Freud had attached to the need for respecting privacy. The person who can succeed in being tactful deserves true diplomatic status.

4

HOW TO LOVE
ANOTHER MAN'S WIFE

....

As a psychotherapist who works not only with individuals, but also with couples, I have witnessed a great deal of marital carnage over the last thirty years. Each week, wives and husbands, long-term girlfriends and boyfriends, as well as gay or lesbian partners, come to my consulting room to complain about the often deep-seated misery which has come to blight their romantic and sexual relationships. Although I sometimes think that I have seen and heard just about every permutation of spousal woe, I soon discover yet another variant of the many ways in which intimate partners can become distanced from one another or even deeply injured by one another.

Over the years, I have encountered many different types of painful, marito-sexual upheavals – whether a wife discovering that her husband might be addicted to Internet pornography; a boyfriend coming to realize that his girlfriend might be lesbian; a man admitting that he has no sexual desire for anyone at all; or a woman confessing that she has reached her seventies without ever having had an enjoyable sexual experience because physical intimacy had always reminded her of early childhood abuse, suffered decades previously at the hands of a close family member. But amid this welter of relational and sexual confusion and distress, two particular symptomatic constellations consume a great deal of my practice, namely:

1. couples who had once enjoyed physical relations prior to marriage but who, upon exchanging rings, no longer find themselves attracted to one another; and
2. long-term partners whose marriages explode in the wake of an extramarital affair.

Perhaps I can offer two representative, clinical illustrations of these phenomena. In order to protect the privacy of those involved, I have changed their forenames, as I have done with all vignettes in this book.

Twenty-six-year-old 'Bertie' and twenty-four-year-old 'Flora' had met at university, and had a very vigorous sex life for five years. They enjoyed one another's company greatly, and eventually married. But within three months of their wedding, their sexual relationship ceased entirely, and neither understood quite why. Bertie expressed the dilemma succinctly: 'The passion just fizzled out one day. It's not that Flora became any less pretty, and it's not like I've put on loads of weight or anything. We just don't fancy each other any more.'

Thirty-five-year-old 'Claude' and his thirty-three-year-old wife 'Greta' had had a very successful marriage for nearly a decade until Claude had become unfaithful, cheating on Greta with 'Irene', the wife of his best friend 'Jamil'. Once again, Greta had no understanding of why Claude felt the need for such infidelity, as she thought that they had a very solid marriage. Claude, too, felt perplexed by his behaviour, as he claimed to love his wife dearly; and yet, he insisted, he simply could not help himself. Also, he could not figure out how he could be so cruel to Jamil – his best buddy – a man who had proved himself to be a loyal friend since boyhood.

Why do human beings struggle so greatly to maintain consistent, ongoing, intimate relationships? Why do we gravitate towards the inhibition of pleasure, as in the case of Bertie and Flora; and why do we harm those we love most, as in the case of Claude, Greta, Irene and Jamil?

Fortunately, Sigmund Freud had some very important insights into the ways in which we undermine our sexual lives and our spousal relationships. Freud had good reason to find answers to these questions. Not only did he encounter cases rather similar to mine in the context of his psychoanalytical clinical practice, but he also strove to find answers, in part because of his own complicated domestic situation. After many years of marriage to his beloved wife Martha, mother of his six children, Freud, by his own admission, ceased all sexual contact with her. Instead, he embarked upon a long-standing affair with his wife's younger sister, Minna Bernays, a spinster who lived in the Freud household, and who had devoted much of her time to the care of his children. We know about the likelihood of this affair from a variety of sources; and in recent years, a sociologist has actually discovered an old hotel register, dating from 1898, which provides evidence that Freud and his sister-in-law had checked into the Schweizerhaus in the Swiss Alps for a holiday. They both stayed overnight in Room 11, and Freud even signed the register 'Dr Sigm Freud u Frau' ('Dr Sigmund Freud and wife').

In 1910, Freud wrote a short but punchy essay entitled 'A Special Type of Choice of Object Made by Men (Contributions to the Psychology of Love I)' which concerns the ways in which our erotic lives can become extremely messy and entangled. Freud noted that we often treat our partners not as *people* but rather, more primitively, as *objects*. As you will see, the terms 'love-object' and 'object-choice' appear throughout:

In the course of psycho-analytic treatment there are ample opportunities for collecting impressions of the way in which neurotics behave in love; while at the same time we can recall having observed or heard of similar behaviour in people of average health or even in those with outstanding qualities. When the material happens to be favourable and thus leads to an accumulation of such impressions, distinct types emerge more clearly. I will begin here with a description of one such type of object-choice – which occurs in men – since it is characterized by a number of 'necessary conditions for loving' whose combination is unintelligible, and indeed bewildering, and since it admits of a simple explanation on psycho-analytic lines.

1. The first of these preconditions for loving can be described as positively specific: wherever it is found, the presence of the other characteristics of this type may be looked for. It may be termed the precondition that there should be 'an injured third party'; it stipulates that the person in question shall never choose as his love-object a woman who is disengaged – that is, an unmarried girl or an unattached married woman – but only one to whom another man can claim right of possession as her husband, fiancé or friend. In some cases this precondition proves so cogent that a woman can be ignored, or even rejected, so long as she does not belong to any man, but becomes the object of passionate feelings immediately she comes into one of these relationships with another man.

2. The second precondition is perhaps a less constant one, but it is no less striking. It has to be found in conjunction with the first for the type to be realized, whereas the first precondition seems very often to occur independently as well. This second precondition is to the effect that a woman who is chaste and whose reputation is irreproachable never exercises an attraction that might raise her to the status of a love-object, but only a woman who is in some way or other of bad repute sexually, whose fidelity and reliability are open to some doubt. This latter characteristic may vary within substantial limits, from the faint breath of scandal attaching to a married woman who is not averse to a flirtation up to the openly promiscuous way of life of a *cocotte* or of an adept in the art of love; but the men who belong to our type will not be satisfied without something of the kind. This second necessary condition may be termed, rather crudely, 'love for a prostitute'.

While the first precondition provides an opportunity for gratifying impulses of rivalry and hostility directed at the man from whom the loved woman is wrested, the second one, that of the woman's being like a prostitute, is connected with the experiencing of *jealousy*, which appears to be a necessity for lovers of this type. It is only when they are able to be jealous that their passion reaches its height and the woman acquires her full value, and they never fail to seize on an occasion that allows them to experience these most powerful emotions.

('A Special Type of Choice of Object Made by Men: (Contributions to the Psychology of Love I)', 1910)

Freud argued that many men become aroused if they can embroil themselves in a relationship with either a *married* woman, or with a taboo, off-limits woman (for example, Freud's sister-in-law) because, in doing so, the man will derive some secret, unconscious, pleasure from the fact that people will be hurt, whether the cuckolded husband, whether the cheating man's wife, or the unfaithful man himself, who runs the risk of being hated by all concerned. Freud also expressed the view that not only do many men enjoy sex with other men's wives, but that many will also find themselves attracted to promiscuous women. By sleeping with a prostitute, a man might derive a secret satisfaction of taking the woman of 'bad repute' away from *all* the other men with whom she has had sexual contact. In this way, the man in question becomes, in his mind, what we might call the 'top dog'.

Freud then proceeded to explain the more deep-seated childhood origins of this particular type of sexual constellation:

psycho-analytic exploration into the life-histories of men of this type has no difficulty in showing that there is such a single source. The object-choice which is so strangely conditioned, and this very singular way of behaving in love, have the same psychical origin as we find in the loves of normal people. They are derived from the infantile fixation of tender feelings on the mother, and represent one of the consequences of that fixation. In normal love only a few characteristics survive which reveal unmistakably the maternal prototype of the object-choice, as, for instance, the preference shown by young men for maturer women; the detachment of libido from the mother has been effected relatively swiftly. In our type, on the other hand, the libido has remained attached to the mother for so long, even after the onset of puberty, that the maternal characteristics remain stamped on the love-objects that are chosen later, and all these turn into easily recognizable mother-surrogates. The comparison with the way in which the skull of a newly born child is shaped springs to mind at this point: after a protracted labour it always takes the form of a cast of the narrow part of the mother's pelvis.

We have now to show the plausibility of our assertion that the characteristic features of our type – its conditions for loving and its behaviour in love – do in fact arise from the psychical constellation connected with the mother. This would seem to be easiest where the first precondition is concerned – the condition that the woman should not be unattached, or that there should be an injured third party. It is at once clear that for the child who is growing up in the family circle the fact of the mother belonging to the father becomes an inseparable part of the mother's essence, and that the injured third party is none other than the father himself. The trait of over-valuing the loved one, and regarding her as unique and irreplaceable, can be seen to fall just as naturally into the context of the child's experience, for no one possesses more than one mother, and the relation to her is based on an event that is not open to any doubt and cannot be repeated.

If we are to understand the love-objects chosen by our type as being above all mother-surrogates, then the formation of a series of them, which seems so flatly to contradict the condition of being faithful to one, can now also be understood.

('A Special Type of Choice of
Object Made by Men: (Contributions to the
Psychology of Love I)', 1910)

So what can we learn from Freud's observations on the psychology of love? Well, first of all, we must discover, yet again, our unconscious vulnerability to damage and sadism in our intimate relationships. As little children, each of us craved the exclusive attention of our mother, or father, or, indeed, of some other primary caregiver. In the classic situation, we each yearned to be our mother's favourite little soldier, or our daddy's girl, for example. But we had to share the limited parental affection with our pesky brothers and sisters, and, worse still, with Mummy's partner – generally the father – or with Daddy's partner – generally the mother. In adult life, we endeavour to repeat this situation – usually unconsciously – by breaking up couples as my client Claude did when he slept with the wife of his best friend Jamil.

But not only do we often succumb to the secret wish to break up someone else's coupling, as Claude and Irene had done by cheating on Greta and Jamil, but sometimes we cannot bear to be in a sexual coupling at all, as happened to my clients Bertie and Flora. Freud would have hypothesized that when we marry, we not only fulfil a long-standing wish to have a special sexual partner, just as Mummy and Daddy had, but, also, we feel sad and guilty that we married the wrong person, someone other than the Mummy or Daddy whom we adored in infancy and early childhood. Thus, many people, upon exchanging wedding rings, feel a conscious sense of pleasure and achievement, but also an unconscious fear of having betrayed the parents, as if to say, 'Look, Mum, I found a woman much better than you,' or 'Hey, Dad, my husband makes more money than you do.' Psychotherapists have come to realize that in order to manage this guilt, couples often desexualize their adult marriages as a means of remaining secretly faithful to their parents. Although such observations may seem complex and even odd, contemporary psychological professionals encounter this dynamic over and over again in our daily work.

With a national divorce rate hovering near 40 per cent, we know only too well how painful and tenuous marriage can be. Freud certainly helped us to understand that the explosions and inhibitions which destroy our intimate partnerships may often occur outside of our conscious awareness or our conscious control. But recognizing that being part of a couple – something for which most of us yearn – may *also* be a source of deep terror, we have the opportunity to seek help if we find ourselves in trouble.

Furthermore, Freud's writings on the psychology of love have the potential to make us aware of the secret desires that might be lurking beneath our conscious lust. Hopefully, the next time we feel erotically tempted by the sight of a married person wearing a shiny gold wedding ring, we might approach this person in a more wary fashion, conscious of the fact that it may be the *ring* (and what it represents, namely the wish to hurt a rival) that attracts us, and the potential for inflicting harm, rather than a curvaceous bosom or a strong pair of biceps. And next time we become uninterested in our own marital partner, we might think about the way in which we may have secretly confused our erotic partner with our caretaking parents of early childhood.

5

HOW TO ERASE YOUR ENTIRE FAMILY ... IN A GOOD WAY

....

Sigmund Freud read books voraciously, and though he immersed himself in many different types of literature, he treasured, above all, the novels, plays, essays and poems of Johann Wolfgang von Goethe, often thought of as Germany's equivalent of William Shakespeare. Freud especially enjoyed Goethe's autobiography, and derived particular insight from one of his memories of an early childhood experience in which, egged on by some companions, Goethe took all of the crockery that he could find in his family's kitchen and threw it out of the window, smashing each piece with gusto.

Although most people would simply dismiss the plate-smashing Goethe as little more than a naughty, mischievous rascal, Freud regarded such childhood memories as very serious pieces of data about the functioning of the human mind; and he suspected that Goethe's frenzied destruction of cups and plates might have a secret symbolic meaning:

In pre-analytic days it was possible to read this without finding occasion to pause and without feeling surprised, but later on the analytic conscience became active. We had formed definite opinions and expectations about the memories of earliest childhood, and would have liked to claim universal validity for them. It should not be a matter of indifference or entirely without meaning which detail of a child's life had escaped the general oblivion. It might on the contrary be conjectured that what had remained in memory was the most significant element in that whole period of life, whether it had possessed such an importance at the time, or whether it had gained subsequent importance from the influence of later events.

The high value of such childish recollections was, it is true, obvious only in a few cases. Generally they seemed indifferent, worthless even, and it remained at first incomprehensible why just these memories should have resisted amnesia; nor could the person who had preserved them for long years as part of his own store of memories see more in them than any stranger to whom he might relate them. Before their significance could be appreciated, a certain work of interpretation was necessary. This interpretation either showed that their content required to be replaced by some other content, or revealed that they were related to some other unmistakably important experiences and had appeared in their place as what are known as 'screen memories'.

('A Childhood Recollection from
Dichtung und Wahrheit', 1917)

In other words, Freud wondered why Goethe had not forgotten this particular incident in the kitchen along with so many other impressions of childhood. Why did this episode remain fresh in his mind? Freud concluded that Goethe's memory actually served as a 'screen' or 'screen memory' for something deeper.

As the eldest of eight children, Sigmund Freud knew a great deal about siblings; and in Goethe, born in 1749, Freud recognized a kindred spirit, knowing that the great German littérateur, also a firstborn child, had to endure the arrival of a gaggle of annoying sisters and brothers; beginning with Cornelia Friederica Christiana in 1750, and followed by Hermann Jakob in 1752, Katharina Elisabetha in 1754, Johanna Maria in 1757 and Georg Adolph in 1760. Freud quickly suspected that when the young Johann Wolfgang von Goethe threw the crockery out of the window, he did so, quite unconsciously, as a disguised means of throwing his sisters and brothers out of the window. But Freud could hardly base a theory of suspected sibling rivalry on one literary reminiscence.

To his delight, Freud came to treat a twenty-seven-year-old patient in psychoanalysis, a young man who, as a child, had also experienced terrific sibling rivalry:

> When he came to me for treatment – by no means the least reason for his coming was that his mother, a religious bigot, had a horror of psycho-analysis – his jealousy of the younger brother (which had once actually been manifested as a murderous attack on the infant in its cradle) had long been forgotten. He now treated his brother with great consideration; but certain curious fortuitous actions of his (which involved sudden and severe injuries to favourite animals, like his sporting dog or birds which he had carefully reared,) were probably to be understood as echoes of these hostile impulses against the little brother.
>
> ('A Childhood Recollection from
> *Dichtung und Wahrheit*', 1917)

This patient bore many similarities to Goethe. Just as Johann Wolfgang had a brother, Hermann Jakob, who arrived some three years after his birth, Freud's patient also had a brother three years his junior. And just as Goethe disposed of all his mother's kitchenware, Freud's patient *also* threw dishes out of the window during childhood. As Freud had discovered, this patient had tried to kill his baby brother, but did not succeed. Instead, the patient attempted to express his sibling hatred by first attacking defenceless animals. But no doubt some grown-up may have stopped him from doing so, and thus, Freud's patient had to find another means of being aggressive; so he, like Goethe, turned to the crockery cupboard:

> The opinion might thus be formed that the throwing of crockery out of the window was a symbolic action, or, to put it more correctly, a *magic* action, by which the child (Goethe as well as my patient) gave violent expression to his wish to get rid of a disturbing intruder. There is no need to dispute a child's enjoyment of smashing things; if an action is pleasurable in itself, that is not a hindrance but rather an inducement to repeat it in obedience to other purposes as well. It is unlikely, however, that it could have been the pleasure in the crash and the breaking which ensured the childish prank a lasting place in adult memory.
>
> ('A Childhood Recollection from *Dichtung und Wahrheit*', 1917)

Freud continued his analysis, suspecting that:

> The pleasure in breaking and in broken things would be satisfied, too, if the child simply threw the breakable object on the ground. The hurling them out of the window into the street would still remain

unexplained. This 'out!' seems to be an essential part of the magic action and to arise directly from its hidden meaning. The new baby must be *got rid of* – through the window, perhaps because he came in through the window. The whole action would thus be equivalent to the verbal response, already familiar to us, of a child who was told that the stork had brought a little brother. 'The stork can take him away again!' was his verdict.

('A Childhood Recollection from *Dichtung und Wahrheit*', 1917)

Some time later, Freud then came to consult with yet another patient who threw objects:

one day I had a patient who began his analysis with the following remarks, which I set down word for word: 'I am the eldest of a family of eight or nine children. One of my earliest recollections is of my father sitting on the bed in his night-shirt, and telling me laughingly that I had a new brother. I was then three and three-quarters years old; that is the difference in age between me and my next younger brother. I know, too, that a short time after (or was it a year before?) I threw a lot of things, brushes – or was it only one brush? – shoes and other things, out of the window into the street. When I was two years old, I spent a night with my parents in a hotel bedroom

at Linz on the way to the Salzkammergut. I was so
restless in the night and made such a noise that my
father had to beat me.

('A Childhood Recollection from
Dichtung und Wahrheit', 1917)

The remarkable biographical similarities which Freud
had gleaned from several patients, as well as from
Goethe's reminiscences, all contributed to the development of a pool of evidence, which helped him to craft
a theory about the widespread nature of sibling rivalry,
and about the way in which we deal with our rivalrous-
ness through symbolic, symptomatic actions.

Freud knew all about death wishes towards siblings.
His mother gave birth to a baby boy, Julius Freud,
shortly after Sigismund Schlomo's first birthday. Julius
died, however, exactly six months later, from dysentery.
At the age of fourteen, the young Sigismund took the
part of the Roman assassin Brutus, in a performance of
a play by Friedrich Schiller, in which he had the opportunity to kill Julius Caesar. Reminiscing about this
experience years later, Freud reflected that:

My emotional life has always insisted that I should
have an intimate friend and a hated enemy. I have
always been able to provide myself afresh with
both, and it has not infrequently happened that the
ideal situation of childhood has been so completely

> reproduced that friend and enemy have come together in a single individual – though not, of course, both at once or with constant oscillations, as may have been the case in my early childhood.
>
> (*The Interpretation of Dreams*, 1900)

In other words, Freud knew that he could be both the Brutus who had begun by befriending Julius (the brother-figure), and also the Brutus who stabs Caesar (the emperor) to death, thus underscoring our tremendous ambivalence towards our loved ones, especially during infancy and childhood.

To the best of our knowledge, Freud never dealt with his early sibling rivalry by throwing Amalia Freud's cups and dishes out of the window of their Vienna apartment, as Johann Wolfgang von Goethe had done during the 1750s, and as Freud's twenty-seven-year-old male patient had done. But Freud did perpetrate at least one act of symbolically throwing the eldest of his five sisters out of the window. His sister Anna Freud (not to be confused with his daughter who would come to bear the same name) played the piano, but apparently the noise disturbed the future psychoanalytical genius so much that he insisted the instrument must go. Already an intellectual prodigy and undoubtedly his mother's favourite, Freud got his wish and managed to have the piano removed from the family flat.

But Freud knew only too well that we do not confine our hatred towards our sisters and brothers; and throughout his vast corpus of writings, he devoted considerable attention to the hostilities that we harbour towards our parents, especially the parent of the opposite sex who prevents us from indulging our secret childhood wish of marrying Mummy or Daddy. When a small Viennese boy called 'Little Hans' came to Freud's office suffering from a phobia of horses, Freud soon deduced that the feared animals served as a substitute for the boy's large, moustachioed father, and that Little Hans wanted to get rid of the father at all costs. Drawing upon the ancient myth of Oedipus who killed his father Laius and bedded his mother Jocasta, Freud referred to Little Hans as a 'little Oedipus' ('Analysis of a Phobia in a Five-Year-Old Boy', 1909), and characterized the Oedipus motif as a 'poetical rendering' ('Fragment of an Analysis of a Case of Hysteria', 1905) which emblematizes much of our early internal life.

Eventually, Freud expanded his references to Oedipus, and coined the phrase 'Oedipus complex' to describe this tragedic constellation which colours our family relationships. He observed that the little boy, in particular

has in fact awakened the memory-traces of the impressions and wishes of his early infancy, and these have led to a reactivation in him of certain mental impulses. He begins to desire his mother herself in the sense with which he has recently become acquainted, and to hate his father anew as a rival who stands in the way of this wish; he comes, as we say, under the dominance of the Oedipus complex. He does not forgive his mother for having granted the favour of sexual intercourse not to himself but to his father, and he regards it as an act of unfaithfulness.

('A Special Type of Choice of
Object Made by Men: (Contributions to the
Psychology of Love I)', 1910)

Freud continued to expand his thinking and he soon came to hypothesize that every boy wishes to kill his father, the original male rival for his mother's affections. Anyone who has ever experienced sexual rivalry during adolescence or adulthood, fearing or knowing that one's beloved might prefer someone else, will have an all-too-painful sense of what Freud had observed.

Biblical descriptions of family life, as well as sentimentalized versions, dictate that we must love our nearest and dearest unconditionally. Sigmund Freud, ever the deconstructing investigator of the domestic arena, suspected that although we love our relatives, we might also, at times, hate them as well, and that to do so might be regarded not as an aberration but as a normality. In fact, in his psychoanalytical consulting room, Freud created a space in which human beings could avail themselves of the opportunity to express their hatred towards their loved ones in words. By recognizing the ordinariness and the omnipresence of hatred in the family sphere, one has licence, through psychotherapy and psychoanalysis, to neutralize the destructive aggressions of family life by transforming that hatred into language, in the confidential presence of the clinician, so that, according to Freud, one can transmogrify one's death threats into frank conversations. Famously, Freud opined that

> the man who first flung a word of abuse at his enemy instead of a spear was the founder of civilization. Thus words are substitutes for deeds, and in some circumstances (e.g. in Confession) the only substitutes.
>
> ('On the Psychical Mechanism of Hysterical
> Phenomena: A Lecture', 1893)

Thus, through the process of psychoanalysis, one may kill off one's hated family members, cathartically, by railing against them in the confessional privacy of the consulting room, thereby hurling verbal lances instead of metallic ones, and consequently transmuting murderous impulses and actions into language.

6

HOW TO KILL A
REALLY FUNNY JOKE

....

Ken Dodd, the famous Liverpudlian comedian, once remarked, quite caustically, 'The trouble with Freud is that he never played the Glasgow Empire Saturday night.' On the whole, we do not think of psychotherapists and psychoanalysts as funny people – quite the opposite, in fact. Spending our days with depressed and anxious people, we have a reputation for being rather joyless. Of course, we do treat our patients or clients very seriously indeed, and we certainly never make jokes at their expense.

Instead of *telling* jokes, those of us in the psychological world *analyse* jokes. And no one psychoanalysed a joke better than Sigmund Freud.

So what did Freud come to understand about jokes? First of all, he differentiated between two types of jokes, firstly, those he referred to as 'innocent' or 'non-tendentious' jokes or riddles which serve no great purpose (for instance, 'Why did the chicken cross the road?'), and secondly, those which carried quite a punch, the so-called 'tendentious' jokes. Freud

regarded the latter variety as potentially quite destructive in nature:

There is, first and foremost, one observation which
warns us not to leave tendentious jokes on one side
in our investigation of the origin of the pleasure we
take in jokes. The pleasurable effect of innocent jokes
is as a rule a moderate one; a clear sense of satisfaction, a slight smile, is as a rule all it can achieve
in its hearers. And it may be that a part even of this
effect is to be attributed to the joke's intellectual
content, as we have seen from suitable examples . . .
A non-tendentious joke scarcely ever achieves the
sudden burst of laughter which makes tendentious
ones so irresistible. Since the technique of both can
be the same, a suspicion may be aroused in us that
tendentious jokes, by virtue of their purpose, must
have sources of pleasure at their disposal to which
innocent jokes have no access.

The purposes of jokes can easily be reviewed.
Where a joke is not an aim in itself – that is, where it
is not an innocent one – there are only two purposes
that it may serve, and these two can themselves
be subsumed under a single heading. It is either a
hostile joke (serving the purpose of aggressiveness,
satire, or defence) or an *obscene* joke (serving the
purpose of exposure). It must be repeated in advance
that the technical species of the joke – whether it is

a verbal or a conceptual joke – bears no relation to these two purposes.

(Jokes and Their Relation to the Unconscious, 1905)

According to Freud, jokes operate most effectively in a highly ritualized situation:

Generally speaking, a tendentious joke calls for three people: in addition to the one who makes the joke, there must be a second who is taken as the object of the hostile or sexual aggressiveness, and a third in whom the joke's aim of producing pleasure is fulfilled. We shall have later to examine the deeper reasons for this state of things; for the moment let us keep to the fact to which this testifies – namely that it is not the person who makes the joke who laughs at it and who therefore enjoys its pleasurable effect, but the inactive listener.

(Jokes and Their Relation to the Unconscious, 1905)

And, once the joke-teller has enlisted the willing ears of the joke-listener in order to lampoon an injured third party, the hostile impulses become expressed through sadistically veiled humour, which cannot find an outlet anywhere else:

Since our individual childhood, and, similarly, since the childhood of human civilization, hostile impulses against our fellow men have been subject to the same restrictions, the same progressive repression, as our sexual urges. We have not yet got so far as to be able to love our enemies or to offer our left cheek after being struck on the right. Furthermore, all moral rules for the restriction of active hatred give the clearest evidence to this day that they were originally framed for a small society of fellow clansmen.

. . .

We are now prepared to realize the part played by jokes in hostile aggressiveness. A joke will allow us to exploit something ridiculous in our enemy which we could not, on account of obstacles in the way, bring forward openly or consciously; once again, then, the joke *will evade restrictions and open sources of pleasure that have become inaccessible.* It will further bribe the hearer with its yield of pleasure into taking sides with us without any very close investigation, just as on other occasions we ourselves have often been bribed by an innocent joke into overestimating the substance of a statement expressed jokingly.

(*Jokes and Their Relation to the Unconscious*, 1905)

In other words, the tendentious, non-innocent joke not only permits the expression of taboo hostile impulses, but it also creates a special pact between the teller and the listener, both of whom reinforce one another's aggressive pleasure by securing their alliance with enjoyable humour.

But how exactly did Freud psychoanalyse a typical joke, and did he take all the fun away with his proto-serious stance? As a nineteenth-century European Jew, born to a struggling merchant, Freud loved jokes about traditional Hebraic customs. He had a particular fondness for jibes about the '*Schadchen*', a Yiddish word for marriage broker or matchmaker, a profession which flourished in previous centuries when parents paid such people to arrange suitable spouses for their children. Let us examine some of Freud's favourite *Schadchen* jokes:

The bridegroom was most disagreeably surprised when the bride was introduced to him, and drew the broker on one side and whispered his remon-strances: 'Why have you brought me here?' he asked reproachfully. 'She's ugly and old, she squints and has bad teeth and bleary eyes ...' – 'You needn't lower your voice', interrupted the broker, 'she's deaf as well.'

(*Jokes and Their Relation to the Unconscious*, 1905)

The bridegroom was paying his first visit to the bride's house in the company of the broker, and while they were waiting in the *salon* for the family to appear, the broker drew attention to a cupboard with glass doors in which the finest set of silver plate was exhibited. 'There! Look at that! You can see from these things how rich these people are.' – 'But', asked the suspicious young man, 'mightn't it be possible that these fine things were only collected for the occasion – that they were borrowed to give an impression of wealth?' – 'What an idea!' answered the broker protestingly. 'Who do you think would lend these people anything?'

(*Jokes and Their Relation to the Unconscious*, 1905)

Reflecting on these sample jokes, Freud commented:

If we bear in mind the fact that tendentious jokes are so highly suitable for attacks on the great, the dignified and the mighty, who are protected by internal inhibitions and external circumstances from direct disparagement, we shall be obliged to take a special view of certain groups of jokes which seem to be concerned with inferior and powerless people. I am thinking of the anecdotes about marriage-brokers, some of which we became acquainted with in the course of our investigation of the various techniques of conceptual jokes. In a few of them, for instance in the examples 'She's deaf as well' ... and 'Who would lend these people anything?' ... the broker is laughed at for his improvidence and thoughtlessness and he becomes comic because the truth escapes him as it were automatically. But does what we have learnt of the nature of tendentious jokes on the one hand and on the other hand our great enjoyment of these stories fit in with the paltriness of the people whom these jokes seem to laugh at? Are they worthy opponents of the jokes? Is it not rather the case that the jokes only put forward the marriage-brokers in order to strike at something more important? Is it not a case of saying one thing and meaning another? It is really not possible to reject this view.

. . .

In any case, if our marriage-broker anecdotes are jokes, they are all the better jokes because, thanks to their façade, they are in a position to conceal not only what they have to say but also the fact that they have something – forbidden – to say. The continuation of this interpretation – and this uncovers the hidden meaning and reveals these anecdotes with a comic façade as tendentious jokes – would be as follows. Anyone who has allowed the truth to slip out in an unguarded moment is in fact glad to be free of pretence. This is a correct and profound piece of psychological insight. Without this internal agreement no one lets himself be mastered by the automatism which in these cases brings the truth to light. But this converts the laughable figure of the *Schadchen* into a sympathetic one, deserving of pity. How happy the man must be to be able at last to throw off the burden of pretence, since he makes use of the first chance of shouting out the very last scrap of truth! As soon as he sees that the case is lost, that the bride does not please the young man, he gladly betrays yet another concealed defect which has escaped notice, or he takes the opportunity of producing an argument that settles a detail in order to express his contempt for the people he is working for: 'I ask you – who would lend these people anything?' The whole of the ridicule in the anecdote now falls upon the parents, barely touched on in it, who think this swindle justified in order to get their daughter a husband.

(*Jokes and Their Relation to the Unconscious*, 1905)

Thus, for Freud, the joke facilitates not only the discharge of socially unacceptable aggressive thoughts and impulses, but it might, also, on occasion, permit the telling of horrible shameful truths.

Returning to Ken Dodd's quip that Freud had never played the Glasgow Empire on a Saturday evening, I suspect that if Freud had had to earn his living as a stand-up comedian, he might well have starved. But by analysing jokes, rather than revelling in them, Freud has given us a unique opportunity to become more conscious of our hidden aggressions as well as our anxieties, helping us to find words for our most painful fears.

While writing this segment, I suddenly recalled a boy from my primary school, someone about whom I have not thought in decades. He developed a reputation as a real class clown, and he told the most shocking jokes. One day, he asked the teacher, 'Excuse me, Miss, why are there no ice cubes in Belfast?' The teacher looked baffled, whereupon the boy replied, 'Because the lady with the recipe died.' Needless to say, the teacher punished this boy for telling an anti-Northern Ireland joke. As I reflect on this years later, I can of course see the cruelty and hostility inherent in the joke, stereotyping the people of Belfast as stupid; but I can also appreciate that the joke conveys the dreadful anxiety that all of us felt as schoolchildren during the 'Troubles' of the 1970s, as witnesses to the unbearably frightening bombings in Central London and elsewhere. Perhaps Freud would have understood the joke as a desperate attempt to process not only this boy's hatred towards the Irish Republican Army but, also, his terror – shared by us all – of being blown up. It would be far more effective to make the Northern Irish into fools who cannot even make ice cubes, rather than accept the reality that a small fringe of IRA terrorists held our lives in their hands.

I would be loath to portray Freud as a humourless person, or indeed to imply that the many mental health professionals who have followed in his footsteps lack playfulness or zest. Being able to have a good chuckle may well represent one of the hallmarks of the mentally healthy personality. Indeed, during the mid-1990s, I had the great pleasure of meeting a very elderly lady called Olga Rosenberg – then more than ninety years of age – whose husband ran a carpet shop in Vienna during the 1930s. She told me a wonderful, unpublished story about Freud. One day, Freud's daughter Anna, herself a noted child psychoanalyst, entered Sandor Rosenberg's carpet shop in search of a gift for her father. Knowing Anna Freud to be the daughter of one of Vienna's most distinguished citizens, Herr Rosenberg offered to deliver the carpet to Freud personally. At their meeting, the carpet merchant told Freud a joke; and though Frau Rosenberg did not recall which joke her husband told Freud, she did remember Freud's delighted reply: '*Das ist ein schöner Witz*' ('That is a beautiful joke').

7

HOW TO FORGET
THE PAST

....

Between the ages of nine and seventeen, the young
Sigismund Schlomo Freud attended the Leopoldstädter
Communal Real- und Obergymnasium school on
Vienna's Taborstraße. During this time he immersed
himself fully in the traditional mid-nineteenth-century
European curriculum, based on a study of the Classics,
especially the language and literature of ancient Greece
and Rome, starting with, among others, Homer, Livy,
Ovid and Xenophon, and progressing to Cicero,
Demosthenes, Horace, Sallust, Tacitus and Virgil. In
order to pass the *Matura* examination – the Viennese
equivalent of our own Advanced Level General Certificate
of Education, though rather more challenging – Freud
had to translate seminal texts from ancient Greek
and Latin into German, including thirty-three lines of
Sophocles's *Oedipus Rex*. His arduous study, to which
he devoted himself with great zeal, kindled a love for
history; and when, as a young physician, Freud began to
earn a salary for his medical consulting work, he would,
from time to time, spend his money acquiring, piece

by piece, a very impressive collection of Greek, Roman, Egyptian, Etruscan, Babylonian, Assyrian, Mycenaean, Mesopotamian, Phoenician, Islamic, Umbrian, Chinese, Japanese and Mexican statuary and other artefacts, which he displayed throughout his apartment, especially in his office.

Any visitor to Freud's consulting room, now carefully preserved in the Freud Museum in London, will be struck quite powerfully by his heaving and priceless collection of more than 2,000 antiquities, which includes statuettes, heads and masks; urns, jars and lamps; amulets, talismans and gems – made variously of marble, terracotta, jade, stone, wood, bronze, metal and glass – and even a fragment of a sarcophagus lid. The objects literally fill the room to capacity with, for example, a first- or second-century Roman bronze statuette of the Greek goddess Athena perched in the centre of Freud's desk; a trio of painted wooden Nineteenth Dynasty Egyptian mummy masks hanging from the bookshelves; and a cast-iron Ming Dynasty head of a bodhisattva, an attendant to the Buddha, nestled on a shelf behind the psychoanalytical couch.

Indeed, Freud confessed to the Austrian writer Stefan Zweig that

despite my much vaunted frugality I have sacrificed a great deal for my collection of Greek, Roman and Egyptian antiquities, have actually read more archaeology than psychology, and that before the war and once after its end I felt compelled to spend every year at least several days or weeks in Rome.

(*The Letters of Sigmund Freud*, 1960)

Freud cluttered his home with these ancient arte-facts partly for aesthetic pleasure but also in order to underscore the value of the faraway past, not only in the history of civilization but within the history of the individual patient as well. Freud compared the psycho-analyst to an archaeologist, excavating the ancient temples of the mind in search of long-forgotten buried treasure – namely, valuable memories, senses, impres-sions and experiences, which had become lost in the mists of repression. As early as 1895, Freud wrote about his newly discovered psychoanalytical treatment method, based, in large measure, on his work with hysterical female patients; and in his description, he underscored a parallel between his own work and that of a digger:

Thus it came about that in this, the first full-length analysis of a hysteria undertaken by me, I arrived at a procedure which I later developed into a regular method and employed deliberately. This procedure was one of clearing away the pathogenic psychical material layer by layer, and we liked to compare it with the technique of excavating a buried city. I would begin by getting the patient to tell me what was known to her and I would carefully note the points at which some train of thought remained obscure or some link in the causal chain seemed to be missing. And afterwards I would penetrate into deeper layers of her memories at these points by carrying out an investigation under hypnosis or by the use of some similar technique. The whole work was, of course, based on the expectation that it would be possible to establish a completely adequate set of determinants for the events concerned.

(Studies on Hysteria, 1895)

By unearthing the hidden past, often secreted intact beneath the rubble of the mind, Freud came to learn that the patient will experience relief and freedom from the ravages of infancy and childhood which remain both forgotten and yet still remembered at the same time, a paradox that the American psychoanalyst Alvin Frank has called 'The Unrememberable and the Unforgettable'.

Intrigued by Heinrich Schliemann's archaeological excavations of ancient Troy, and of Arthur Evans's discoveries of the palace at Knossos on the island of Crete, Freud revelled in the study of antiquity and archaeology, and he often spoke to his patients about the importance of digging up the past – slowly and gently, of course – in order to retrieve the pathogenic memories of early childhood abuse in a safe manner. One of Freud's male patients, for example, presented with a hysterical paralysis of his foot, for which no neurological explanation could be found. Amid the course of psychoanalytical treatment, Freud discovered that during the patient's childhood, a grown woman had forced him to stimulate her genitals with his foot, and this experience proved so traumatic that in later life the man unconsciously anaesthetized his own foot in order to prevent any such reoccurrence, hence its hysterical paralysis.

Freud believed that the scarabs and beads and pots and flasks which filled his office conveyed precious information about the past in exactly the same way in which the patient's free associations, generated while lying on the couch, could inform the psychotherapist or psychoanalyst about the origins and meanings of the patient's symptoms, character structure, inhibitions and dreams. Freud's patient the 'Wolf Man' (thus named because of a seminal lupine dream) recalled Freud pontificating that 'the psychoanalyst, like the archaeologist in his excavations, must uncover layer after layer of the patient's psyche, before coming to the deepest most valuable treasures'.

Indeed, Freud argued vehemently that one can never forget one's past, and that like archaeological ruins, some relics of our ancient personal history will remain for ever in our mind:

Since we overcame the error of supposing that the forgetting we are familiar with signified a destruction of the memory-trace – that is, its annihilation – we have been inclined to take the opposite view, that in mental life nothing which has once been formed can perish – that everything is somehow preserved and that in suitable circumstances (when, for instance, regression goes back far enough) it can once more be brought to light. Let us try to grasp what this assumption involves by taking an analogy from another field. We will choose as an example the history of the Eternal City. Historians tell us that the oldest Rome was the *Roma Quadrata*, a fenced settlement on the Palatine. Then followed the phase of the *Septimontium*, a federation of the settlements on the different hills; after that came the city bounded by the Servian wall; and later still, after all the transformations during the periods of the republic and the early Caesars, the city which the Emperor Aurelian surrounded with his walls. We will not follow the changes which the city went through any further, but we will ask ourselves how much a visitor, whom we will suppose to be equipped with the most complete historical and topographical knowledge, may still find left of these early stages in the Rome of to-day. Except for a few gaps, he will see the wall of Aurelian almost unchanged. In some places he will be able to find sections of the Servian wall where they have been excavated and brought to light. If he knows enough – more than present-day archaeology does – he may perhaps be able to trace out in the plan of the city the whole course of that wall and the outline of the *Roma Quadrata*. Of the buildings which once occupied this ancient area he will find nothing, or only scanty remains, for they exist no longer. The best information about Rome in the republican era would only enable him at the most to point out the sites where the temples and public buildings of that period stood. Their place is now taken by ruins, but not by ruins of themselves but of later restorations made after fires or destruction. It is hardly necessary to remark that all these remains of ancient Rome are found dovetailed into the jumble of a great metropolis which has grown up in the last few centuries since the Renaissance. There is certainly not a little that is ancient still buried in the soil of the city or beneath its modern buildings. This is the manner in which the past is preserved.

(*Civilization and its Discontents*, 1930)

Freud also realized that each of us might have several layers of our mind on display at the same time. For instance, every grown-up has the capacity to be both extremely mature at work, but also quite childlike back at home with their partner. Similarly, if one visits the Forum Romanum in Italy, one readily observes that several different chapters of ancient civilization appear before us simultaneously.

Freud expanded the analogy between the map of ancient Rome and the map of the human mind:

Now let us, by a flight of imagination, suppose that Rome is not a human habitation but a psychical entity with a similarly long and copious past – an entity, that is to say, in which nothing that has once come into existence will have passed away and all the earlier phases of development continue to exist alongside the latest one. This would mean that in Rome the palaces of the Caesars and the Septizonium of Septimius Severus would still be rising to their old height on the Palatine and that the castle of S. Angelo would still be carrying on its battlements the beautiful statues which graced it until the siege by the Goths, and so on. But more than this. In the place occupied by the Palazzo Caffarelli would once more stand – without the Palazzo having to be removed – the Temple of Jupiter Capitolinus; and this not only in its latest shape, as the Romans of the Empire saw it, but also in its earliest one, when it still showed Etruscan forms and was ornamented with terracotta antefixes. Where the Coliseum now stands we could at the same time admire Nero's vanished Golden House. On the Piazza of the Pantheon we should find not only the Pantheon of to-day, as it was bequeathed to us by Hadrian, but, on the same site, the original edifice erected by Agrippa; indeed, the same piece of ground would be supporting the church of Santa Maria sopra Minerva and the ancient temple over which it was built. And the observer would perhaps only have to change the direction of his glance or his position in order to call up the one view or the other.

(Civilization and its Discontents, 1930)

Shortly before his death, Freud provided us with his most explicit analogy yet of the psychoanalyst as an archaeologist of the mind:

His work of construction, or, if it is preferred, of reconstruction, resembles to a great extent an archaeologist's excavation of some dwelling-place that has been destroyed and buried or of some ancient edifice. The two processes are in fact identical, except that the analyst works under better conditions and has more material at his command to assist him, since what he is dealing with is not something destroyed but something that is still alive – and perhaps for another reason as well. But just as the archaeologist builds up the walls of the building from the foundations that have remained standing, determines the number and position of the columns from depressions in the floor and reconstructs the mural decorations and paintings from the remains found in the débris, so does the analyst proceed when he draws his inferences from the fragments of memories, from the associations and from the behaviour of the subject of the analysis. Both of them have an undisputed right to reconstruct by means of supplementing and combining the surviving remains. Both of them, moreover, are subject to many of the same difficulties and sources of error. One of the most ticklish problems that confronts the archaeologist is notoriously the determination of the relative age of his finds; and if an object makes its appearance in some particular level, it often remains to be decided whether it belongs to that level or whether it was carried down to that level owing to some subsequent disturbance. It is easy to imagine the corresponding doubts that arise in the case of analytic constructions.

('Constructions in Analysis', 1937)

As a psychotherapist, I spend a great deal of my working life helping patients to think about their childhood and its impact. Many people suffer from parental bereavements, painful punishments, crushing humiliations and other adverse experiences, and may, also, have enjoyed tender affection from mother or father, or the joys of happy play with siblings and friends. Some of us revisit childhood in our mind, celebrating the healthy peaks, and crying about the debilitating troughs. But other people place a repressive blanket over childhood, pretending that toxic events never happened. I find that such people often suffer from great anger, resentment and rage in adult life, still nursing early wounds which have never healed. Fortunately, Freud has helped us to recognize the importance of childhood and of its excavation.

Freud revelled in the Latin aphorism *Saxa loquuntur*, 'the stones speak' ('The Aetiology of Hysteria', 1896), a phrase that he may well have noticed while walking through the Sigmundstor or Sigmund's door, an eighteenth-century tunnel in Salzburg which, as it happens, bears his forename. By relishing the archaeological excavation of the mind, and by resurrecting repressed memories, Freud taught us a vital life lesson, namely, that we cannot, and must not, forget the past. It impacts upon us whether we wish it to do so or not; and thus we have an obligation to explore our childhood in the hope of putting our ghosts in the nursery to rest.

8

HOW TO BE COMPLETELY
INCONSEQUENTIAL

....

According to show-business lore, the film star and cabaret artiste Marlene Dietrich had a notorious reputation for egotism. Once, after a live concert performance, Dietrich assembled a group of fawning admirers in her dressing room and enquired, rather disingenuously: 'Didn't I sing that first song well? And didn't I look great in the red dress? And didn't I get a big laugh after telling that joke? ... But enough about me, what did *you* think of my performance?'

In 1914, Sigmund Freud wrote a seminal essay, 'On Narcissism: An Introduction', in which he provided a very clear description of the clinical phenomenon of people who become completely self-obsessed and convinced of their own importance. Freud regarded the narcissist as infantile, and as someone who believes himself or herself to be the centre of the universe, much like the neonate who has neither the capacity nor the need to express concern about others.

Every baby begins life as an omnipotent narcissist. The newborn craves food and, lo and behold, a breast appears, as if by magic, full of tasty milk. The newborn infant feels a chill and then, equally impressively, a blanket appears, seemingly from nowhere, offering warmth. These early experiences of being cared for by a diligent parent allow the little girl or boy to develop what Freud called 'primary narcissism', a healthy and necessary stage of development which places the infant's physical and psychological needs at the fore-front. Good parents do not mind too much if the infant behaves like a diva-in-training; after all, young boys and girls have neither the motoric skills nor the cognitive capacities to cook their own supper or to dress themselves. Parents must become servants, providing twenty-four-hour room service catering for the infant's every requirement, in order for the child to survive.

But while most of us become more independent and self-reliant as we age, some people never renounce the narcissistic attitude of babyhood, and they become clinical narcissists in adult life, whose relentless self-absorption causes grievous offence to family and friends and work colleagues. Freud came to regard the adult narcissist as psychologically troubled, noting that:

> The term narcissism is derived from clinical description . . . to denote the attitude of a person who treats his own body in the same way in which the body of a sexual object is ordinarily treated – who looks at it,

that is to say, strokes it and fondles it till he obtains complete satisfaction through these activities. Developed to this degree, narcissism has the significance of a perversion that has absorbed the whole of the subject's sexual life, and it will consequently exhibit the characteristics which we expect to meet with in the study of all perversions.

('On Narcissism: An Introduction', 1914)

As most of us grow older, we learn to share space with others, starting with our siblings and our schoolmates. We arrive at the painful realization that other children may have birthday parties, other boys and girls also score 100 per cent in the arithmetic exam, and so forth. But many people who suffer from a deep sense of inadequacy and deprivation cannot abandon this early narcissistic posture, and they persist, Dietrich-like, in stealing the limelight. Freud noted that:

Observation of normal adults shows that their former megalomania has been damped down and that the psychical characteristics from which we inferred their infantile narcissism have been effaced.

. . .

We have learnt that libidinal instinctual impulses undergo the vicissitude of pathogenic repression if they come into conflict with the subject's cultural and ethical ideas. By this we never mean that the individual in question has a merely intellectual knowledge of the existence of such ideas; we always mean that he recognizes them as a standard for himself and submits to the claims they make on him.

('On Narcissism: An Introduction', 1914)

Freud realized that narcissists cannot bear the ordinariness of their lives, and thus they often lament:

Why did not Nature give us the golden curls of Balder or the strength of Siegfried or the lofty brow of genius or the noble profile of aristocracy? Why were we born in a middle-class home instead of in a royal palace? We could carry off beauty and distinction quite as well as any of those whom we are now obliged to envy for these qualities.

('Some Character-Types Met with in Psycho-Analytic Work', 1916)

In order to become emotionally healthy grown-ups, we must abandon our infantile narcissism, and find a way to become less grandiose, less self-centred and better able to share our planet with 7 billion other people. In other words, we must also learn to become *inconsequential,* and to accept the fact that life has other meanings and sources of satisfaction than the pursuit of fame and glory, and of having statues built in our honour.

But Freud went further in his understanding of the nature of inconsequentiality. Not only did he underscore the importance of divesting ourselves of our infantile narcissism – of our need to be the star of the show – but, also, he further shattered the narcissistic illusions of humankind by claiming that human beings in general may not be quite as impressive as we suspect.

Freud knew only too well that most people regard themselves as independent agents, controlling their own lives, determining their destinies, choosing their careers and their partners carefully; but he argued that although we pretend to be the architects of our existence, we do, in fact, become slaves to powerful unconscious forces which govern our minds and our behaviours. Throughout his psychoanalytical writings, Freud came to describe himself (perhaps a tad narcissistically) as a great revolutionary in history who shattered the narcissistic illusions of human beings. He positioned himself as the most recent in a trinity of geniuses, along with Nicolaus Copernicus, the sixteenth-century astronomer, and Charles Darwin, the nineteenth-century evolutionist – rather impressive company. Freud summarized his epic observations thus:

I propose to describe how the universal narcissism of men, their self-love, has up to the present suffered three severe blows from the researches of science.

a. In the early stages of his researches, man believed at first that his dwelling-place, the earth, was the stationary centre of the universe, with the sun, moon and planets circling round it. In this he was naïvely following the dictates of his sense-perceptions, for he felt no movement of the earth, and wherever he had an unimpeded view he found himself in the centre of a circle that enclosed the external world. The central position of the earth, moreover, was a token to him of the dominating part played by it in the universe and appeared to fit in very well with his inclination to regard himself as lord of the world.

The destruction of this narcissistic illusion is associated in our minds with the name and work of Copernicus in the sixteenth century. But long before his day the Pythagoreans had already cast doubts on the privileged position of the earth, and in the third century BC Aristarchus of Samos had declared that the earth was much smaller than the sun and moved round that celestial body. Even the great discovery of Copernicus, there-fore, had already been made before him. When this discovery achieved general recognition, the self-love of mankind suffered its first blow, the *cosomological* one.

b. In the course of the development of civilization man acquired a dominating position over his fellow-creatures in the animal kingdom. Not content with this supremacy, however, he began to place a gulf between his nature and theirs. He denied the possession of reason to them, and to himself he attributed an immortal soul, and made claims to a divine descent which permitted him to break the bond of community between him and the animal kingdom. Curiously enough, this piece of arrogance is still foreign to children, just as it is to primitive and primaeval man. It is the result of a later, more pretentious stage of development.

. . .

We all know that little more than half a century ago the researches of Charles Darwin and his collaborators and fore-runners put an end to this presumption on the part of man. Man is not a being different from animals or superior to them; he himself is of animal descent, being more closely related to some species and more distantly to others. The acquisitions he has subsequently made have not succeeded in effacing the evidences, both in his physical structure and in his mental disposi-tions, of his parity with them. This was the second, the *biological* blow to human narcissism.

c. The third blow, which is psychological in nature, is probably the most wounding.

Although thus humbled in his external rela-tions, man feels himself to be supreme within his own mind. Somewhere in the core of his ego he has developed an organ of observation to keep a watch on his impulses and actions and see whether they harmonize with its demands.

. . .

But, these two discoveries – that the life of our sexual instincts cannot be wholly tamed, and that mental processes are in themselves unconscious and only reach the ego and come under its control through incomplete and untrustworthy perceptions – these two discoveries amount to a statement that *the ego is not master in its own house*. Together they represent the third blow to man's self-love, what I may call the *psychological* one. No wonder, then, that the ego does not look favourably upon psycho-analysis and obstinately refuses to believe in it.

('A Difficulty in the Path of
Psycho-Analysis', 1917)

Copernicus forced us to realize that the earth revolves around the sun. Darwin helped us to recognize that we cannot trace our ancestry back to Adam and Eve. And Freud insisted that we do not control our own minds. These three revolutions constitute an overwhelming attack on the narcissistic concept of man as centre of the universe.

The experience of being a grandiose baby, who comes to regard himself or herself as the exalted child of a deity, and who believes the planet earth to be the best address in the universe, may be pleasurable at some level. But eventually, in order to come to terms with the life that we do have as ordinary, hard-working, ageing people of finite means and capacities, we must abandon our infantile, megalomaniacal, narcissistic self-image, and learn how to be one of billions of fellow citizens, in a large solar system, all of whom will one day die. As Freud explained:

> Just as a planet revolves around a central body as well as rotating on its own axis, so the human individual takes part in the course of development of mankind at the same time as he pursues his own path in life. But to our dull eyes the play of forces in the heavens seems fixed in a never-changing order; in the field of organic life we can still see how the forces contend with one another, and how the effects of the conflict are continually changing. So, also, the two urges, the one towards personal happiness and the other towards union with other human beings, must struggle with each other in every individual; and so, also, the two processes of individual and of cultural development must stand in hostile opposition to each other and mutually dispute the ground.
>
> (*Civilization and its Discontents*, 1930)

In order to be mentally healthy, one must aspire towards greater creativity of course, but, similarly, one must also come to accept the fact that however brilliant one's paintings, poetry, musical compositions or scientific experiments; however stunning one's face and figure; however large one's wallet; someone else will always outdo us. Freud observed that when confronted with great writers such as Rudyard Kipling, Mark Twain and Émile Zola, inter alia, we cannot avoid 'the feeling of one's own smallness in the face of their greatness' ('Contribution to a Questionnaire on Reading', 1906). Furthermore, we must come to recognize that even if we do write better than William Shakespeare or paint better than Leonardo da Vinci, we remain but mortal, specks of dust in an increasingly expanding galaxy.

Copernicus and Darwin, and most especially Freud, can help us to conquer our hubris and our self-importance, and assist us in embracing our *insignificance* in the universe. In doing so, we will have the opportunity to enjoy lives of greater modesty, with scope for more realistic achievement and less fantastic failure.

CONCLUSION:
FREUD'S
HUMANITARIAN LEGACY

....

Many psychologists have come to regard Sigmund Freud as outdated, as a male chauvinist pig, or even as a liar. So why has he earned everlasting greatness, and why should we turn to this long-deceased, cigar-smoking, grey-haired, balding old man for enlightenment about our modern lives?

First and foremost, Freud became the spearhead for a revolution in the care and treatment of those people suffering from deep psychological distress, the so-called 'mentally ill'. During antiquity, it would not be uncommon for 'crazy' people to be murdered, in part because they could not contribute usefully to their community, and in part because they frightened people who had no idea how to be of assistance to them. In Tudor times, mad people would be chained and beaten, fed rats (quite literally), or burned at the stake as witches. And during the early nineteenth century, mad people would be dropped into holes in the floors of their homes and left to fester. Modern-day mental health workers would blush with deep shame to realize how cruelly our professional predecessors treated their patients in previous centuries. In the last quarter of the nineteenth century, when Freud attended medical school, doctors would not only incarcerate lunatics for life in very decrepit, unhygienic institutions, but they would even perform vicious and unnecessary surgeries on the mad, which included castration of the testicles for men suffering from 'dementia praecox' (what we now refer to as schizophrenia), and cauterization or excision of the clitoris for women diagnosed as 'hysteric'. If any twenty-first-century physician or psychologist offered such treatments, he or she would be imprisoned in perpetuity in Broadmoor Hospital for the criminally insane.

Freud engineered a profoundly paradigm-shifting approach to the treatment of psychological *dis*-ease. He invited his patients to recline comfortably on a sofa in his tastefully furnished, confidential consulting room, and he offered them an opportunity to talk without interruption, and encouraged them to reveal the secrets – often sexually traumatic secrets – which had plagued their minds for decades. In doing so, Freud not only developed, as we know, the first substantial hands-*off* approach to healing in the history of medicine, but he created a form of psychiatric treatment which did not require potions or pills; instead, Freud offered a psychoanalytical approach which required good listening and deep compassion for human suffering. By allowing his patients to talk, and to narrate their stories, Freud discovered that his earliest patients experienced a deep catharsis – relief from a whole host of symptoms which had tormented them for years and years.

Additionally, Freud deployed his psychoanalytical art in a very unusual way. Unlike other physicians of the late nineteenth and early twentieth centuries who practised medicine in a deeply patrician manner, and who always wore a white laboratory coat, Freud abandoned this traditional garb, opting instead for a plain three-piece suit. Similarly, unlike his contemporaries who often incarcerated their patients in lunatic asylums which afforded absolutely no privacy, Freud developed a confidential setting in which his patients could articulate their most shameful or aggressive thoughts; and he promised his patients that no one else would ever come to know about the private content of their minds. And Freud never sat behind a desk as other physicians would have done; instead, he positioned himself in a chair right next to the couch on which his patients lay so that he could hear them well, and could be close to them. In some ways, he took the best of medicine, and the best of the Catholic confessional, mixed them together, and created a de-medicalized, de-theologized form of treatment in which neither doctor nor priest became the ultimate authority. Instead, Freud placed the patient and his or her narrative at the centre of this healing enterprise, and he allowed his patients to speak what previously had remained unspoken. He elevated raw communication above the scalpel and the X-ray; and he foregrounded understanding instead of penance and self-flagellation as a cure for one's sins. In many respects, he created a huge transformation in the nature of human relationships, prioritizing privacy, frankness, compassion, tolerance, destigmatization and intimacy above all else. Consequently, Freud deserves to be remembered as a great humanitarian.

Freud has great relevance still, not only for the mental health worker but also for all sentient people who wish to understand more about their lives. By sculpting a psychology of the unconscious, Freud has helped us to appreciate a great deal about the deep complexities of our mind, both its erotic and aggressive aspects, as well as our wish for close human contact and our subsequent fear of intimacy.

He taught us all a vast amount about our potential for destruction – a potential that we deny at every turn. And yet, as Freud demonstrated, our envy, our hostility and our hatred seep out, quite unconsciously, catching us off guard, causing embarrassment to ourselves and others, and sometimes, deep pain and cruelty as well. By becoming more aware of the hidden infantile and childhood origins of our adult thoughts, behaviours and fantasies, and by recognizing that most of this material remains hidden in the depths of our unconscious mind, Freud bequeathed to us a rich, detailed and provocative psychology which, once absorbed, has the ability to improve our sensitivity to ourselves and others, to deepen our creativities, and to enhance the fabric of our lives.

We can of course lampoon Sigmund Freud as a bourgeois fuddy-duddy who spent too much time thinking about his sister-in-law, but if we dismiss his lifetime of unrelenting research into the origin and amelioration of human torment, we do so at our own peril.

HOMEWORK

INTRODUCTION

....

Sigmund Freud wrote so many books, essays and letters that students often struggle to know how best to tackle this mountain of Freudiana. Without doubt, James Strachey's magisterial translation, *The Standard Edition of the Complete Psychological Works of Sigmund Freud* (1953–74), undertaken in collaboration with Anna Freud, Alix Strachey and Alan Tyson – an unparalleled work of scholarship in twenty-four volumes – remains the best starting point. *The Psychopathology of Everyday Life: Forgetting, Slips of the Tongue, Bungled Actions, Superstitions and Errors*, contained in Volume VI, may be the most accessible entrée for those who have not previously read any Freud. As for Freud's letters, Ernst Falzeder's meticulous edition of *The Complete Correspondence of Sigmund Freud and Karl Abraham: 1907–1925, Completed Edition* (2002) cannot be bettered.

For a more personal glimpse into the life of Freud, the brief, but highly readable, memoir *Freud: Master and Friend* (1944), by leading disciple Hanns Sachs, and the equally engaging *My Analysis with Freud: Reminiscences* (1977), by Freud's analysand Abram Kardiner, never fail to delight. And Michael Molnar's superbly scholarly edition of Freud's private chronicle, *The Diary of Sigmund Freud: 1929–1939, A Record of the Final Decade* (1992), provides the reader with ongoing rewards.

Freud has given rise to an immense biographical literature. Though much criticized nowadays as too hagiographical, Ernest Jones's three-volume study, *The Life and Work of Sigmund Freud – Volume 1: The Formative Years and the Great Discoveries, 1856–1900* (1953); *Volume 2: Years of Maturity, 1901–1919* (1955); and *Volume 3: The Last Phase, 1919–1939* (1957) – remains my favourite survey of his life, not only for its first-hand, eyewitness account of crucial events but also for its fine literary merits. Thereafter, I would recommend the many stimulating books by leading Freud historian Paul Roazen, most especially *Freud and His Followers* (1975) and *Meeting Freud's Family* (1993). Sander Gilman's excellent and erudite works on Freud brilliantly contextualize the man in a Central European and Jewish context, especially *Freud, Race, and Gender* (1993), *The Case of Sigmund Freud: Medicine and Identity at the Fin de Siècle* (1993), and *Reading Freud's Reading* (1994), co-edited by Jutta Birmele, Jay Geller and Valerie D. Greenberg. George Makari has written undoubtedly the most profound history of Freud's psychoanalytical movement, *Revolution in Mind: The Creation of Psychoanalysis* (2008); and Lisa Appignanesi and John Forrester have produced a sterling book on

Freud's Women (1992), which counterbalances some of the traditional characterizations about Freud and gender. Finally, for deeply serious and intelligent critical studies of Freud one can do no better than Peter L. Rudnytsky's penetrating work, *Rescuing Psychoanalysis from Freud and Other Essays in Re-vision* (2011), and Mikkel Borch-Jacobsen and Sonu Shamdasani's bold and frank tome, *The Freud Files: An Inquiry into the History of Psychoanalysis* (2012).

1
HOW TO SABOTAGE YOUR GREATEST SUCCESS

....

Search any good art history book and immerse yourself in the painting of Napoleon Bonaparte on horseback, crossing the Alps, by Jacques-Louis David, completed circa 1800–03. Or better yet, pop over to the Château de Malmaison, outside Paris, to see the original version of this magnificent canvas of beauty and bombast. David's oil painting, commonly entitled *Bonaparte franchissant le Grand-Saint-Bernard*, might serve as a useful reminder of the way in which Napoleon, having conquered much of Europe, then exploded all of his efforts when, at the peak of his potency, he launched his wildly unsuccessful Russian campaign. Most of us will never conquer a European country in our lifetime, but we might, nonetheless, benefit from being reminded of Napoleon's explosive act of self-destruction.

2
HOW TO MAKE A MOUNTAIN OUT OF A MOLEHILL

....

Google a video called 'Political Freudian Slips', posted on YouTube. This amusing, though chilling, collection of Freudian slips about noted political figures will offer a sobering warning about the way in which our unconscious mind betrays our deeper wishes and sentiments. This video of political parapraxes includes a reference to Governor Sarah Palin as Governor *Failin'*.

3
HOW TO BETRAY A DEEP, DARK SECRET

....

More than 6,000 years ago, physicians in ancient Greece began to swear an oath of ethical practice. Attributed to the physician Hippocrates, and known still today as the Hippocratic Oath, it contains a pledge to preserve the secrets of any patient with whom one works. Search out a copy of the Hippocratic Oath in a medical library or online, and study it carefully. One common translation of the oath contains the following promise: 'Whatever, in connection with my professional service, or not in connection with it, I see or hear, in the life of men, which ought not to be spoken of abroad, I will not divulge, as reckoning that all such should be kept secret.' Keeping this oath in mind may be of great value, and will earn the respect of family, friends and colleagues.

4
HOW TO LOVE ANOTHER MAN'S WIFE

....

Few playwrights have understood the complexities of marital psychology as well as Harold Pinter. The next time someone mounts a production of his 1978 drama *Betrayal*, rush to see it; or, in the interim, read a copy of the script. Pinter portrays the destructiveness of the sexless marriage and of the extramarital affair with such psychological veracity that one would be tempted to think he might have read much Freud in his spare time.

5
HOW TO ERASE YOUR ENTIRE FAMILY ...
IN A GOOD WAY

....

Carve out some time to read a wonderful nineteenth-century novel, *La Cousine Bette* (*Cousin Bette*), written by the highly psychologically perceptive author Honoré de Balzac, a marvellous account of an embittered woman who plots to kill off many of the members of her family with cunning and subterfuge and, quite chillingly, with a sense of self-justification. Balzac's novel, first published in 1846, has a frightening contemporaneity, and serves as a warning about what might happen when family grievances cannot be aired.

6
HOW TO KILL A REALLY FUNNY JOKE

....

Many years ago, I heard an amusing riddle: 'How can you spot a psychiatrist at the Folies Bergère?' 'He's the one studying the audience.' Although this may not be the most humorous of pleasantries, it certainly underscores the point that a psychological professional not only participates in the general culture, but also endeavours to observe it from the outside as well. For your homework assignment, go to a live comedy event, and instead of absorbing yourself solely in the comedian, perhaps you might try to study the audience and begin to hypothesize why people laugh at certain jokes. After a short while, you may well discover that Freud had a point when he concluded that we often laugh in order to discharge aggression. See if you can identify *any* jokes which do not make fun of someone in a potentially hostile manner. You may well be hard-pressed to do so.

7
HOW TO FORGET THE PAST

....

Interview an elderly relative, preferably a parent or grandparent, about your earliest infancy. Ask your relative what he or she remembers about you as a baby or as a little boy or girl. You may find yourself surprised to learn that much had happened to you about which you have no conscious memories. The deeper you probe, the more you may uncover. This homework assignment requires, of course, a basic trust in your interviewee, as well as the knowledge that one may terminate the interview at any time, depending upon the sort of information that might emerge.

8
HOW TO BE COMPLETELY INCONSEQUENTIAL
....

Watch a DVD of *Planet of the Apes*, the 1968 American film based on Pierre Boulle's novel, *La Planète des singes*, first published in 1963. Alternatively, one might wish to read John Wyndham's novel *The Day of the Triffids*, which appeared in 1951, or view the eponymous 1962 film adaptation. Both of these works of literature and cinema remind us very powerfully that human beings may not necessarily be the masters or mistresses of the universe, a realization that we must increasingly embrace as we live in the perilous shadow of global warming.

ACKNOWLEDGEMENTS

....

I wish to express my warm thanks to Alain de Botton for his unique and visionary work in having created the School of Life, and to Morgwn Rimel, its Director, for her bold and tireless leadership. I must also express my deep appreciation to my wonderful colleague Jane Wynn Owen, the Associate Director of the Psychotherapy Service, and to all the Staff Psychotherapists at the School of Life, for their wisdom and devotion. Caroline Brimmer, Mary Toal, Harriet Warden and the other School of Life staff, past and present, deserve my further gratitude.

John Armstrong provided helpful advice about this manuscript, and Juliette Mitchell has earned everlasting kudos as the most agreeable and efficient of project managers. Cindy Chan, my editor at Pan Macmillan, has proved to be the most felicitous of readers, and her benevolent shepherding and her many sagacious suggestions have contributed greatly to this book.

I also wish to acknowledge my friends and colleagues at the Freud Museum in London for their passionate, though non-idolatrous, dedication to the preservation and furtherance of Freud's work over many long years.

My family, and most especially my wife Kim, teaches me new life lessons all the time, for which I offer love and thanks.